BE STRONG

Be Strong

WARREN W. WIERSBE

While this book is intended for the reader's personal enjoyment and profit, it is also intended for group study. A leader's guide with Reproducible Response Sheets is available from your local bookstore or from the publisher.

VICTOR BOOKS

A DIVISION OF SCRIPTURE PRESS PUBLICATIONS INC.
USA CANADA ENGLAND

Copyediting: Jerry Yamamoto and Barbara Williams
Cover Design: Grace Chan
Cover Photo: Allstock

Library of Congress Cataloging-in-Publication Data

Wiersbe, Warren W.
    Be strong / by Warren W. Wiersbe.
       p.   cm.
    ISBN 1-56476-122-3
    1. Bible. O.T. Joshua—Criticism, interpretation, etc.
    2. Spiritual warfare. I. Title.
    BS1295.2.W54 1993
    222'.206—dc20   93-3197
                                    CIP

---

1 2 3 4 5 6 7 8 9 10 Printing/Year 97 96 95 94 93

CONTENTS

PREFACE

An author takes a risk writing a book about war at a time in history when war in general, and "religious wars" in particular, are detested, and when some Christian denominations are removing the "militant" songs from the church hymnal.

But I'll take that risk, because I think the church needs the message of the Book of Joshua more than ever before. We're living in a day of reproach and defeat, and the church is no longer "clear as the sun, and terrible as an army with banners" (Song 6:10). We look more like a bunch of prisoners of war.

Whether we like it or not, God's people are expected to be soldiers. At least Paul thought so: "You therefore must endure hardship as a good soldier of Jesus Christ. No one engaged in warfare entangles himself with the affairs of this life, that he may please him who enlisted him as a soldier" (2 Tim. 2:3-4, NKJV).

The Book of Joshua tells us how to be victorious soldiers and how to claim our rich spiritual inheritance in Jesus Christ. It tells us how to be strong and courageous as we face our enemies and march forward to claim new territory for the Lord.

In his farewell speech to the American Congress, April 19, 1951, General Douglas MacArthur said, "In war there is no substitute for victory." General Joshua would have agreed with him; and in his book, he shows us the way to victory.

I hope you will follow—by faith.

Warren W. Wiersbe

A Suggested Outline of the Book of Joshua

Theme: Claiming our victory and our inheritance in Christ
Theme verse: Joshua 1:8

I. Preparing the Nation — 1–5
   1. Encouraging the leader — 1
   2. Spying out the land — 2
   3. Crossing the river — 3–4
   4. Affirming the covenant — 5

II. Defeating the Enemy — 6–12
   1. The Central campaign — 6–9
   2. The Southern campaign — 10
   3. The Northern campaign — 11
   4. Summary of the victories — 12

III. Claiming the Inheritance — 13–22
   1. Territory assigned to the tribes — 13–19
   2. Cities of refuge set apart — 20
   3. Cities for the Levites identified — 21
   4. Border tribes sent home — 22

IV. Renewing the Covenant — 23–24
   1. Joshua's final message to the leaders — 23
   2. Joshua's final message to the nation — 24

ONE

INTRODUCTION TO THE BOOK OF JOSHUA

A New Beginning

Why should anybody today study the Book of Joshua, an ancient book that gives a grim account of war, slaughter, and conquest? If the Book of Joshua were fiction, we might accept it as an exciting adventure story; but the book conveys real history and is a part of inspired Holy Scripture. What does it mean to us today?

"There never was a good war, or a bad peace," Benjamin Franklin wrote in 1783; but it's possible that the wise old patriot was wrong for once. After all, God called Joshua to be a general and to lead the army of Israel in holy conquest. *But there were bigger issues involved in that conquest than the invasion and possession of a land—issues that touch our lives and our faith today.*

That's why we're embarking on this study. The Book of Joshua is the book of new beginnings for the people of God, and many believers today need a new beginning. After forty years of wandering in the wilderness, Israel claimed their inheritance and enjoyed the blessings of the land that God had prepared for them, "as the days of heaven upon the earth" (Deut. 11:21). That's the kind of life God wants us to experience today. Jesus Christ, our Joshua, wants to lead us in conquest *now* and share with us all the treasures of His wonderful inheritance. He has "blessed us with all spiritual blessings" (Eph. 1:3), but too often we live like defeated paupers.

1. The new leader

From Exodus 3 to Deuteronomy 34, the Bible focuses attention on the ministry of Moses, God's chosen servant to lead the nation of Israel. But Moses died; and though he would not be forgotten (he's named over fifty times in the Book of Joshua), a new "servant of the Lord" (Josh. 24:29) would take his place. "God buries His workers, but His work goes on." We shall note later that this change in leadership carries with it a tremendous spiritual lesson for believers who want to experience God's best in their lives.

Joshua the slave. God spent many years preparing Joshua for his calling. He was born into slavery in Egypt and was given the name Hoshea (Num. 13:8), which means "salvation." Moses later changed it to Joshua (v. 16, NIV), "Jehovah is salvation," which is the Hebrew form of "Jesus" (Matt. 1:21; see Acts 7:45 and Heb. 4:8). When his parents gave the baby the name "salvation," they were bearing witness to their faith in God's promise of redemption for His people (Gen. 15:12-16; 50:24-26). Joshua belonged to the tribe of Ephraim and was the firstborn son of Nun (1 Chron. 7:20-27). This meant that his life was in danger the night of Passover, but he had faith in the Lord and was protected by the blood of the lamb (Ex. 11–12).

While in Egypt, Joshua saw all the signs and wonders that God performed (Ex. 7–12); and he knew that Jehovah was a God of power who would care for His people. The Lord had humiliated the gods of Egypt and demonstrated that He alone was the true God (Ex. 12:12; Num. 33:4). Joshua saw the Lord open the Red Sea and then close the waters and drown the pursuing Egyptian army (Ex. 14–15). Joshua was a man of faith who knew the Lord and trusted Him to do wonders for His people.

Joshua the soldier. The first official recorded act of Joshua in Scripture is his defeat of the Amalekites when they attacked Israel about two months after Israel's exodus from Egypt (17:8-16). Moses was a prophet and legislator, but Joshua was a general with exceptional military skills. He was also a man of great courage, who wasn't afraid to confront the enemy and trust the Lord for victory.

Where did Joshua learn to use a sword and to command an army? Certainly he was especially gifted by the Lord, but even heavenly gifts must be discovered and developed in an earthly setting. Had Joshua in some way been involved with the Egyptian army and received his early training in its ranks? This is possible, though the Scriptures are silent and we must not be dogmatic. Just as Moses refused a high position in Pharaoh's palace but received his education there (Heb. 11:24-26; Acts 7:22), so Joshua may have turned down army promotions that he might identify with his people and serve the Lord.

According to Exodus 17:14, the writer suggests that God had chosen Joshua for a special work in the future. Unknown to Joshua, the battle with Amalek was a testing time when God was examining his faith and courage. "Make every occasion a great occasion, for you can never tell when someone may be taking your measure for a larger place" (Marsden). Joshua's conflict with Amalek was the preparation for many battles he would fight in the Promised Land.

Joshua the servant. In Exodus 24:13, Joshua is called Moses' servant ("minister"), which indicates that Joshua was now an official assistant to the leader of Israel. He accompanied Moses to the mount and went with him when he judged the people for making the golden calf (32:17). It wasn't enough that Joshua be a good warrior; he also had to know the God of Israel and the holy laws God gave His people to obey. We shall discover that the secret of Joshua's victories was not his skill with the sword but his submission to the Word of God (Josh. 1:8) and to the God of the Word (5:13-15).

During Israel's wilderness journey, Moses had a special tent set up outside the camp where he could meet with God (Ex. 33:7-11). It was Joshua's responsibility to stay at the tent and guard it. Not only was Joshua a warrior, but he was also a worshiper and knew how to live in the presence of God.

Joshua was jealous not only for the glory of God but also for the honor and authority of Moses. This is a good characteristic for a servant to have, and it showed up when God sent His Spirit upon the seventy elders Moses had chosen to assist him in his work (Num. 11:16-30). When the Spirit came upon Eldad and Medad in the camp, two men who had not assembled with the other elders at the tabernacle, Joshua protested and asked Moses to stop them from prophesying. (For a New Testament parallel, see Luke 9:49-50.) The breadth of Moses' spirit must have moved Joshua as Moses claimed no special privileges for himself. It's worth noting that when the inheritance was allotted after the conquest of the Promised Land, Joshua took his share last (Josh. 19:49-51).

Joshua the spy. When Israel arrived at Kadesh Barnea, on the border of the Promised Land, God commanded Moses to appoint twelve men to spy out the land of Canaan—Joshua among them (Num. 13). After forty days of investigating the land, the spies returned to Moses and reported that the land was indeed a good one. But ten of the spies discouraged the people by saying that Israel wasn't strong enough to overcome the enemy, while two of the spies—Caleb and Joshua—encouraged the people to trust God and move into the land. Sadly the people listened to the faithless ten spies. It was this act of unbelief and rebellion that delayed the conquest of the land for forty years.

This crisis revealed some fine leadership qualities in Joshua. He was not blind to the realities of the situation, but he didn't allow the problems and difficulties to rob him of his faith in God. The ten spies looked at God through the difficulties, while Joshua and Caleb looked at the difficulties through what they knew about God. Their God was big enough for the battles that lay ahead!

Knowing he was right, Joshua wasn't afraid to stand up against the majority. He, Moses, and Caleb stood alone and risked their lives in so doing; *but God stood with them.* It has well been said that "one with God is a majority." It would take that kind of courage for Joshua to lead Israel into their land so they could defeat their enemies and claim their inheritance.

Think of the years of blessing in the Promised Land that Joshua forfeited because the people had no faith in God! But Joshua patiently stayed with Moses and did his job, knowing that one day he and Caleb would get their promised inheritance (Num. 14:1-9). Leaders must know not only how to win victories but also how to accept defeats. I have a suspicion that Joshua and Caleb met each other regularly and encouraged each other as the time of their inheritance drew near. Day after day, for forty years, they saw the older generation die off, but each day brought them closer to Canaan. (See Heb. 10:22-25 for a New Testament parallel.)

Joshua the successor. Throughout that wilderness journey, God was preparing Joshua for his ministry as successor to Moses. When Israel defeated Og, king of Bashan, Moses used that victory to encourage Joshua not to be afraid of his enemies (Deut. 3:21-28; Num. 21:33-35). When Moses was preparing to die, he asked God to give the people a leader; and God appointed Joshua (27:12-23; Deut. 3:23-29). In his final message to Israel, Moses told the people that God would use Joshua to defeat their enemies and help them claim their promised inheritance; and he also encouraged Joshua to trust God and not be afraid (31:1-8). Moses laid hands on Joshua and God imparted to Joshua the spiritual power he needed for his task (34:9).

Like Moses, Joshua was human and made his share of mistakes; but he was still God's chosen and anointed leader, and the people knew this. This is why they said to Joshua, "Just as we heeded Moses in all things, so we will heed you" (Josh. 1:17, NKJV). God's people in the church today need to acknowledge God's leaders and give them the respect that they deserve as the servants of God (1 Thes. 5:12-13).

The secret of Joshua's success was his faith in the Word of God (Josh. 1:7-9), its commandments and its promises. God's Word to Joshua was "Be strong!" (vv. 6-7, 9, 18; and see Deut. 31:6-7, 23); and this is His Word to His people today.

2. The new land

The promise of the land. The word "land" is found eighty-seven times in the Book of Joshua because this book is the record of Israel's entering, conquering, and claiming the Promised Land. God promised to give the land to Abraham (Gen. 12:1-7; 13:15-17; 15:7, 18; 17:8; 24:7), and He reaffirmed the promise to Isaac (26:1-5), Jacob (28:4, 13, 15; 35:12), and their descendants (50:24). The Exodus narrative gives many reaffirmations of the promise (3:8, 17; 6:4, 8; 12:25; 13:5, 11; 16:35; 23:20-33; 33:1-3; 34:10-16), and these are repeated in Leviticus (14:34; 18:3; 19:23; 20:22-24; 23:10; 25:2, 38) and Numbers (11:12; 15:2, 18; 16:13-14; 20:12, 24; 27:12; 33:53; 34:2, 12). (See also 1 Chron. 16:14-18.)

In Moses' "farewell speech" (Deut.), he frequently mentioned the land and the nation's responsibility to possess it. The word "land" is found nearly 200 times in Deuteronomy and the word "possess" over 50 times. Israel *owned* the land because of God's gracious covenant with Abraham (Gen. 12:1-5), but their *enjoyment* of the land depended on their faithful obedience to God. (See Lev. 26 and Deut. 28–30.) As long as the Jews obeyed God's law He blessed them, and they prospered in the land. But when they turned from God to idols, God first chastened them *in the land* (the Book of Judges); and then He took them *from their land* to the land of Babylon. After they had been chastened for seventy years, Israel returned to their land; but they never fully recovered the glory and blessing that they once had known.

God called the Promised Land "a good land" (8:7-10) and contrasted it with the monotony and barrenness of Egypt (11:8-14). It was to be Israel's place of rest, her inheritance, and the dwelling place of God (12:9, 11). After enduring slavery in Egypt and misery in the wilderness, the Jews would finally find rest in their Promised Land (Josh. 1:13, 15; 11:23; 21:44; 22:4; 23:1). This concept of "rest" will show up again in Psalm 95:11 and Hebrews 4 as an illustration of the victory Christians can have if they give their all to the Lord.

The Prophet Ezekiel called the land of Israel "the glory of all lands" (Ezek. 20:6, 15), which the NIV translates "the most beautiful of all lands." Daniel calls it "the pleasant land" (8:9) and "the glorious land" (11:16 and 41). Often it is described as "a land flowing with milk and honey" (Ex. 3:8, 17; 13:5; 33:3; Lev. 20:24; Num. 13:27; Deut. 6:3; 11:9; etc.). This was a proverbial statement meaning "a land of plenty," a place of peaceful pastures and gardens where the herds could graze and the bees could gather pollen and make honey.

The importance of the land. The Prophet Ezekiel said that Jerusalem was "in the center of the nations" (5:5, NIV) and that the land of Israel was "the center of the world" (38:12, NASB). The Hebrew word translated "center" also means "navel," suggesting that Israel was the "lifeline" between God and this world; for "salvation is of the Jews" (John 4:22). *God chose the land of Israel to be the "stage" on which the great drama of redemption would be presented.*

In Genesis 3:15, God promised to send a Savior to the world; and the first step in the fulfilling of that promise was the call of Abraham. Beginning with Genesis 12, the Old Testament record focuses on the Jews and the land of Israel. Abraham left Ur of the Chaldees to go to that new land, and there Isaac and Jacob were born. God announced that the Redeemer would come from the tribe of Judah (49:10) and the family of David (2 Sam. 7). He would be born of a virgin in Bethlehem (Isa. 7:14; Micah 5:2) and one day die for the sins of the world (Isa. 53; Ps. 22). All these important events in the drama of redemption would take place in the land of Israel, the land that Joshua was called to conquer and claim.

3. The new life

It's unfortunate that some of our Christian songs have equated Israel's crossing the Jordan with the believer's dying and going to heaven, because this mistake brings confusion when you start interpreting the Book of Joshua. "Swing Low, Sweet Chariot" is a beloved spiritual, but I fear its imagery is not biblical. The hymn "On Jordan's Stormy Banks" perpetuates that same error, as does the third verse of "Guide Me, O Thou Great Jehovah":

> When I tread the verge of Jordan,
> Bid my anxious fears subside;
> Death of death, and hell's destruction,
> Land me safe on Canaan's side.
>
> (William Williams)

The events recorded in the Book of Joshua have to do with the *life* of God's people and not their *death!* The Book of

A NEW BEGINNING

Joshua records battles, defeats, sins, and failures—none of which will take place in heaven. This book illustrates how believers today can say good-bye to the old life and enter into their rich inheritance in Jesus Christ. It explains how we can meet our enemies and defeat them, and how to claim for ourselves all that we have in Jesus Christ (Eph. 1:3). What Paul's letter to the Ephesians explains doctrinally, the Book of Joshua illustrates practically. It shows us how to claim our *riches* in Christ.

But it also shows us how to claim our *rest* in Christ. This is one of the major themes of the Book of Hebrews and is explained in chapters 3 and 4 of that epistle. In those chapters, we find four different "rests," all of which are related: God's Sabbath rest after creating the worlds (Heb. 4:4; Gen. 2:2); the salvation rest we have in Christ (Heb. 4:1, 3, 8-9; Matt. 11:28-30); the believer's eternal rest in heaven (Heb. 4:11); and the rest God gave Israel after their conquest of Canaan (3:7-19).

God's promise to Moses was "My Presence will go with you, and I will give you rest" (Ex. 33:14, NKJV). The Jews certainly had no rest in Egypt or during their wilderness wanderings; but in the Promised Land, God would give them rest. In his farewell message to the people, Moses said, "For as yet you have not come to the rest and the inheritance which the Lord your God is giving you" (Deut. 12:9, NKJV; and see 3:20; 12:9-10; 25:19). *This "Canaan rest" is a picture of the rest that Christian believers experience when they yield their all to Christ and claim their inheritance by faith.*

The four geographic locations seen in the history of Israel illustrate four spiritual experiences. *Egypt* was the place of death and bondage from which Israel was delivered. They were delivered from death by the blood of the lamb and from bondage by the power of God who opened the Red Sea and took them across safely. This illustrates the salvation we

17

have through faith in Jesus Christ, "The Lamb of God who takes away the sin of the world!" (John 1:29, NKJV) Through His death and resurrection, Jesus Christ delivers the believing sinner from bondage and judgment.

The wilderness experience of Israel depicts believers who live in unbelief and disobedience and don't enter into the rest and riches of their inheritance in Christ, either because they don't know it's there or they know and refuse to enter. Like Israel, they come to a crisis place (Kadesh Barnea), but refuse to obey the Lord and claim His will for their lives (Num. 13–14). They are delivered from Egypt, but Egypt is still in their hearts; and like the Jews, they have a desire to go back to the old life (Ex. 16:1-3; Num. 11; 14:2-4; see Isa. 30:3; 31:1). Instead of marching through life as conquerors, they meander through life as wanderers and never enjoy the fullness of what God has planned for them. It's this crowd that is especially addressed in the Epistle to the Hebrews.

Canaan represents the Christian life as it ought to be: conflict and victory, faith and obedience, spiritual riches and rest. It's a life of faith, trusting Jesus Christ, our Joshua, the Captain of our salvation (Heb. 2:10), to lead us from victory to victory (1 John 5:4-5). When Israel was in Egypt, the enemy was *around* them, making their lives miserable. When they crossed the Red Sea, Israel put the enemy *behind* them; but when the nation crossed the Jordan River, they saw new enemies *before* them, and they conquered these enemies by faith.

The victorious Christian life isn't a once-for-all triumph that ends all our problems. As pictured by Israel in the Book of Joshua, the victorious Christian life is a series of conflicts and victories as we defeat one enemy after another and claim more of our inheritance to the glory of God. The eminent Scottish preacher Alexander Whyte used to say that the victorious Christian life was "a series of new beginnings."

A NEW BEGINNING

According to Joshua 11:23, the whole land was taken; but according to 13:1, there remained "very much land to be possessed." Is this a contradiction? No, it's the declaration of a basic spiritual truth: In Christ, we have all that we need for victorious Christian living, but we must possess our inheritance by faith, a step at a time (Josh. 1:3), a day at a time. Joshua's question to his people is a good question to ask the church today: "How long will you wait before you begin to take possession of the land that the Lord . . . has given you?" (18:3, NIV)

The fourth geographic location on Israel's "spiritual map" is *Babylon,* where the nation endured seventy years of captivity because they disobeyed God and worshiped the idols of the pagan nations around them. (See 2 Chron. 36; Jer. 39:8-10). When God's children are willfully rebellious, their loving Father must chasten them until they learn to be submissive and obedient (Heb. 12:1-11). When they confess their sins and forsake them, God will forgive and restore His children to fellowship and fruitfulness (1 John 1:9; 2 Cor. 7:1).

The leading person in the Book of Joshua is not Joshua but the Lord Jehovah, the God of Joshua and of Israel. In all that Joshua did by faith, he desired to glorify the Lord. When the Jews crossed the Jordan River, Joshua reminded them that the living God was among them and would overcome their enemies (Josh. 3:10). Through Israel's obedience, Joshua wanted all the people of the earth to know the Lord and fear Him (4:23-24). In his "farewell addresses" to the leaders (chap. 23) and to the nation (chap. 24), Joshua gave God all the glory for what Israel had accomplished under his leadership.

At least fourteen times in this book, God is called "the Lord God of Israel" (7:13, 19-20; 8:30; 9:18-19; 10:40, 42; 13:14, 33; 14:14; 22:24; 24:2, 23). *Everything that Israel did brought either glory or disgrace to the name of their God.* When

Israel obeyed by faith, God kept His promises and worked on their behalf; and God was glorified. But when they disobeyed in unbelief, God abandoned them to their own ways and they were humiliated in defeat. The same spiritual principle applies to the church today.

As you look at your life and the life of the church where you fellowship, do you see yourself and your fellow believers wandering in the wilderness or conquering in the Promised Land? In the wilderness, the Jews were a complaining people; but in Canaan, they were a conquering people. In the wilderness, Israel kept looking back, yearning for what they had in Egypt; but in the Promised Land, they looked forward to conquering the enemy and claiming their rest and their riches. The wilderness march was an experience of delay, defeat, and death; but their experience in Canaan was one of life, power, and victory.

As you look at the "spiritual map" of your Christian life, where are you living?

Follow the Leader

Twice during my years of ministry, I've been chosen to succeed distinguished and godly leaders and carry on their work. I can assure you that it wasn't easy to follow well-known Christians who sacrificially poured years of their lives into successful ministries. I can identify with Joshua when he stepped into Moses' sandals and discovered how big they were!

When I succeeded D.B. Eastep as pastor of Calvary Baptist Church in Covington, Kentucky, I remember how his widow and his son encouraged me and assured me of their support. I recall one of the deacons, George Evans, coming to the church office to tell me he would do anything to help me, "including washing your car and polishing your shoes." I never asked George to do either of those things, but his words expressed the encouraging attitude of all the church staff and leaders. I felt like a raw recruit taking the place of a seasoned veteran, and I needed all the help I could get!

Nearly a quarter of a century later when I succeeded Theodore Epp at Back to the Bible, I had a similar experience. The board and headquarters staff, the leaders in the overseas offices, the radio listeners, as well as many Christian leaders from all over the world, assured me of their prayer support and availability to help. When you feel like a midget taking the place of a giant, you appreciate all the encouragement God sends your way.

What a new leader needs is not advice but encouragement. "To encourage" literally means "to put heart into." General Andrew Jackson said "one man with courage makes a majority," and he was right. As God's people today face the challenges that God gives us, we would do well to learn from the threefold encouragement found in this chapter.

1. God encourages His leader (Josh. 1:1-9)

Encouragement from God's commission (vv. 1-2). Leaders don't lead forever, even godly leaders like Moses. There comes a time in every ministry when God calls for a new beginning with a new generation and new leadership. Except for Joshua and Caleb, the old generation of Jews had perished during the nation's wanderings in the wilderness; and Joshua was commissioned to lead the new generation into a new challenge: entering and conquering the Promised Land. "God buries His workmen, but His work goes on." It was God who had chosen Joshua, and everybody in Israel knew that he was their new leader.

Over the years I've seen churches and parachurch ministries flounder and almost destroy themselves in futile attempts to embalm the past and escape the future. Their theme song was, "As it was in the beginning, so shall it ever be, world without end." Often I've prayed with and for godly Christian leaders who were criticized, persecuted, and attacked simply because, like Joshua, they had a divine commission to lead a ministry into new fields of conquest; but the people would not follow. More than one pastor has been offered as a sacrificial lamb because he dared to suggest that the church make some changes.

22

FOLLOW THE LEADER

J. Oswald Sanders writes: "A work originated by God and conducted on spiritual principles will surmount the shock of a change of leadership and indeed will probably thrive better as a result" *(Spiritual Leadership,* p. 132).

In describing the death of King Arthur, Lord Tennyson put some wise and profound words in the mouth of the king as his funeral barge moved out to sea. Sir Bedevire cried out, "For now I see the true old times are dead"; and Arthur replied:

> The old order changeth, yielding place to new,
> And God fulfills himself in many ways,
> Lest one good custom should corrupt the world.
> ["The Passing of Arthur"]

"Would that life were like the shadow cast by a wall or a tree," says the *Talmud,* "but it is like the shadow of a bird in flight." Trying to clutch the past to our hearts is as futile as trying to embrace the passing shadow of a bird in flight.

A wise leader doesn't completely abandon the past but builds on it as he or she moves toward the future. Moses is mentioned fifty-seven times in the Book of Joshua, evidence that Joshua respected Moses and what he had done for Israel. Joshua worshiped the same God that Moses had worshiped, and he obeyed the same Word that Moses had given to the nation. There was continuity from one leader to the next, but there wasn't always conformity; for each leader is different and must maintain his or her individuality. Twice in these verses Moses is called God's servant, but Joshua was also the servant of God (24:29). The important thing is not the servant but the Master.

Joshua is called "Moses' minister" (1:1), a word that described workers in the tabernacle as well as servants of a leader. (See Ex. 24:13; 33:11; Num. 11:28; Deut. 1:38.) Joshua learned how to obey as a servant before he commanded as a general; he was first a servant and then a ruler (Matt. 25:21). "He who has never learned to obey cannot be a good commander," wrote Aristotle in his *Politics.*

God commissioned Joshua to achieve three things: lead the people into the land, defeat the enemy, and claim the inheritance. God could have sent an angel to do this, but He chose to use a man and give him the power he needed to get the job done. As we have already seen, Joshua is a type of Jesus Christ, the Captain of our salvation (Heb. 2:10), who has won the victory and now shares His spiritual inheritance with us.

Encouragement from God's promises (vv. 3-6). Since Joshua had a threefold task to perform, God gave him three special promises, one for each task. God would enable Joshua to cross the river and claim the land (vv. 3-4), defeat the enemy (v. 5), and apportion the land to each tribe as its inheritance (v. 6). God didn't give Joshua explanations as to *how* He would accomplish these things, because God's people live on promises and not on explanations. When you trust God's promises and step out by faith (v. 3), you can be sure that the Lord will give you the directions you need when you need them.

First, God promised Joshua that *Israel would enter the land (vv. 3-4).* Over the centuries God had reaffirmed this promise, from His first words to Abraham (Gen. 12) to His last words to Moses (Deut. 34:4). God would take them over the Jordan and into enemy territory. He then would enable them to claim for themselves the land that He had promised them. There would be no repetition of the fear and unbelief that had brought the nation into defeat at Kadesh Barnea (Num. 13).

God had already given them the land; it was their responsibility now to step out by faith and claim it (Josh 1:3; see Gen. 13:14-18). The same promise of victory that God had given to Moses (Num. 11:22-25), He reaffirmed to Joshua; and He

24

carefully defined the borders of the land. Israel didn't reach that full potential until the reigns of David and Solomon.

The lesson for God's people today is clear: God has given us "all spiritual blessings . . . in Christ" (Eph. 1:3), and we must step out by faith and claim them. He has set before His church an open door that nobody can close (Rev. 3:8), and we must walk through that door by faith and claim new territory for the Lord. *It is impossible to stand still in Christian life and service; for when you stand still, you immediately start going backward.* "Let us go on!" is God's challenge to His church (Heb. 6:1), and that means moving ahead into new territory.

God also promised Joshua *victory over the enemy (Joshua 1:5).* The Lord told Abraham that other nations were inhabiting the Promised Land (Gen. 15:18-21), and He repeated this fact to Moses (Ex. 3:17). If Israel obeyed the Lord, He promised to help them defeat these nations. But He warned His people not to compromise with the enemy in any way, for then Israel would win the war but lose the victory (23:20-33). Unfortunately, that's exactly what happened. Since the Jews began to worship the gods of their pagan neighbors and adopt their evil practices, God had to chasten Israel in their land to bring them back to Himself (Jud. 1–2).

What a promise God gave to Joshua! "As I was with Moses, so I will be with you; I will never leave you or forsake you" (Josh 1:5, NIV). God had given a similar promise to Jacob (Gen. 28:15), and Moses had repeated God's promise to Joshua (Deut. 31:1-8). God would one day give this same promise to Gideon (Jud. 6:16) and to the Jewish exiles returning from Babylon to their land (Isa. 41:10; 43:5); and David would give it to his son Solomon (1 Chron. 28:20). But best of all, *God has given this promise to His people today!* The Gospel of Matthew opens with "Emmanuel . . . God with us" (1:23) and closes with Jesus saying, "Lo, I am with you always" (28:20, NKJV). The writer of Hebrews 13:5 quotes Joshua 1:5 and applies it to Christians today: "I will never leave you nor forsake you" (NKJV).

This means that God's people can move forward in God's will and be assured of God's presence. "If God be for us, who can be against us?" (Rom. 8:31) Before Joshua began his conquest of Jericho, the Lord appeared to him and assured him of His presence (Josh. 5:13-15). That was all Joshua needed to be guaranteed of victory.

When my wife and I were in our first pastorate, God led the church to build a new sanctuary. The congregation was neither large nor wealthy, and a couple of financial experts told us it couldn't be done; but the Lord saw us through. He used 1 Chronicles 28:20 in a special way to strengthen and assure me throughout that difficult project. I can assure you from experience that the promise of God's presence really works!

(3) God's third promise to Joshua was that *He would divide the land as an inheritance for the conquering tribes (Josh. 1:6).* This was God's assurance that the enemy would be defeated and that Israel would possess their land. God would keep His promise to Abraham that his descendants would inherit the land (Gen. 12:6-7; 13:14-15; 15:18-21).

The Book of Joshua records the fulfillment of these three promises: the first in chapters 2–5, the second in chapters 6–12, and the third in chapters 13–22. At the close of his life Joshua could remind the leaders of Israel that "not one thing has failed of all the good things which the Lord your God spoke concerning you. All have come to pass for you; not one word of them has failed" (23:14, NKJV).

Before God could fulfill His promises, however, Joshua had to exercise faith and "be strong and of good courage" (1:6). Divine sovereignty is not a substitute for human responsibility. God's sovereign Word is an encouragement to God's servants to believe God and obey His commands. As Charles

Spurgeon put it, Joshua "was not to use the promise as a couch upon which his indolence might luxuriate, but as a girdle wherewith to gird up his loins for future activity" *(Metropolitan Tabernacle Pulpit,* vol. 14, p. 97). In short, God's promises are prods, not pillows.

Encouragement from God's written Word (vv. 7-8). It's one thing to say to a leader, "Be strong! Be very courageous!" and quite something else to enable him to do it. Joshua's strength and courage would come from meditating on the Word of God, believing its promises, and obeying its precepts. This was the counsel Moses had given to all the people (Deut. 11:1-9), and now God was applying it specifically to Joshua.

During the years of his leadership, Moses kept a written record of God's words and acts and committed this record to the care of the priests (Deut. 31:9). He wrote in it a reminder to Joshua to wipe out the Amalekites (Ex. 17:14). Among other things, the "Book of the Law" included "the Book of the Covenant" (24:4, 7), a record of the journeys of the people from Egypt to Canaan (Num. 33:2), special regulations dealing with inheritance (36:13), and the song that Moses taught the people (Deut. 31:19). Moses kept adding material to this record until it included everything God wanted in it (v. 24). We have reason to believe the entire five Books of Moses (Genesis through Deuteronomy) comprised "the Book of the Law," the greatest legacy Moses could leave to his successor.

But it wasn't enough for the priests to carry and guard this precious book; Joshua had to take time to read it daily and make it a part of his inner person by meditating on it (Ps. 1:2; 119:97; see Deut. 17:18-20). The Hebrew word translated "meditate" means "to mutter." It was the practice of the Jews to read Scripture aloud (Acts 8:26-40) and talk about it to themselves and to one another (Deut. 6:6-9). This explains why God warned Joshua that the Book of the Law was not to depart out of his *mouth* (Josh. 1:8). In numerous conferences, I have often told pastors and seminary students, "If you don't talk to your Bible, your Bible isn't likely to talk to you!"

In the life of the Christian believer, *prosperity* and *success* aren't to be measured by the standards of the world. These blessings are the by-products of a life devoted to God and His Word. If you set out on your own to become prosperous and successful, you may achieve your goal and *live to regret it.* "In whatever man does without God," wrote Scottish novelist George MacDonald, "he must fail miserably, or succeed more miserably." The questions God's people need to ask are: Did we obey the will of God? Were we empowered by the Spirit of God? Did we serve to the glory of God? If we can answer yes to these questions, then our ministry has been successful in God's eyes, no matter what people may think.

Encouragement from God's commandment (v. 9). God's commandments are still God's enablements for those who obey Him by faith. Gabriel's words to Mary are as true today as when he spoke them in Nazareth: "For with God nothing shall be impossible" (Luke 1:37). I especially like the translation of this verse found in the *American Standard Version* (1901): "For no word from God shall be void of power." The very word that God speaks has in it the power of fulfillment if we will but trust and obey!

In the years to come, whenever Joshua faced an enemy and was tempted to be *afraid,* he would remember that he was a man with a divine commission—and his fears would vanish. Whenever things went wrong and he was tempted to be *dismayed,* he would recall God's command—and take new courage. Like Moses before him, and Samuel and David after him, Joshua had a divine mandate to serve the Lord and do His will—and that mandate was sufficient to carry him through.

2. The leader encourages the officers (Josh. 2:10-15)

The nation of Israel was so organized that Moses could quickly communicate with the people through his officers who formed a chain of command (Deut. 1:15). Moses didn't assemble the leaders to ask for their advice but to give them God's orders. There are times when leaders must consult with their officers, but this was not one of them. God had spoken, His will was clear, and the nation had to be ready to obey.

Forty years before, at Kadesh Barnea, the nation had known the will of God but refused to obey it (Num. 13). Why? Because they believed the report of the ten spies instead of believing the commandment of God and obeying by faith. Had they listened to Caleb and Joshua—the minority report—they would have spared themselves those difficult years of wandering in the wilderness. There is a place in Christian service for godly counsel, but a committee report is no substitute for the clear commandment of God.

Instead of the command to prepare food, you would have expected Joshua to say, "Prepare boats so we can cross the Jordan River." Joshua didn't try to second-guess God and work things out for himself. He knew that the God who opened the Red Sea could also open the Jordan River. He and Caleb had been present when God delivered the nation from Egypt, and they had confidence that God would work on their behalf again.

Though he trusted God for a miracle, Joshua still had to prepare for the everyday necessities of life. In modern armies the Quartermaster Corps sees to it that the soldiers have food and other necessities of life; but Israel didn't have a Quartermaster Corps. Each family and clan had to provide its own food. The manna was still falling each morning (Ex. 16) and wouldn't stop until Israel was in their land (Josh. 5:11-12). But it was important that the people stayed strong because they were about to begin a series of battles for possession of their Promised Land.

Note that Joshua's words to his leaders were words of faith and encouragement. "You shall pass over! You shall possess the land! The Lord will give it to you!" Joshua had made a similar speech forty years before, but that generation of leaders wouldn't listen. Now that generation was dead and the new generation was ready to believe God and conquer the land.

It's unfortunate but true that sometimes the only way a ministry can move forward is by conducting a few funerals. A pastor friend of mine pleaded with his church board to build a new educational plant to house an exploding Sunday School. One of the long-time members of the board, a prominent businessman in the city, said to him, "You'll do this over my dead body!" *And they did!* A few days later, that officer had a heart attack and died; and the church moved ahead and built the much-needed educational plant.

The older we get, the more danger there is that we'll get set in our ways and become "sanctified obstructionists"; *but it doesn't have to happen.* Caleb and Joshua were the oldest men in the camp, and yet they were enthusiastic about trusting God and entering the land. It isn't a matter of *age;* it's a matter of *faith;* and faith comes from meditating on the Word of God (1:8; Rom. 10:17). How I thank God for the "senior saints" who have been a part of my ministry and have encouraged me to trust the Lord and move forward.

Joshua had a special word for the two and a half tribes that lived on the other side of Jordan and had already received their inheritance (Num. 32). He reminded them of Moses' words of instruction and warning (21:21-35; Deut. 3:12-20) and urged them to keep the promise they had made. Joshua was concerned that Israel be a *united* people in conquering the land and in worshiping the Lord. The two and a half tribes did keep their promise to help conquer the land, but they still created a problem for Joshua and Israel because they lived on the other side of the Jordan (Josh. 22).

In the nation of Israel it was the able men twenty years and older who went out to war (Num. 1:3); and the record shows that the two and a half tribes had 136,930 men available (26:7, 18, 34). But only 40,000 men actually crossed the Jordan and fought in the Promised Land (Josh. 4:13). The rest of the recruits stayed to protect the women and children in the cities the tribes had taken in the land of Jazer and the land of Gilead (32:1-5, 16-19). When the soldiers returned home, they shared the spoils of war with their brothers (Josh. 22:6-8).

It was a concession on Moses' part to allow the two and a half tribes to live outside the Promised Land. The tribes liked the land there because it was "a place for cattle" (Num. 32:1, 4, 16). Apparently their first concern was making a living, not making a life. They would rather have big flocks and herds than dwell with their brothers and sisters in the inheritance God had given them. They were far from the place of worship and had to erect a special monument to remind their children that they were citizens of Israel (Josh. 22:10ff). They represent the many "borderline believers" in the church today who get close to the inheritance but never quite claim it, no matter how successful they may seem to be. They are willing to serve the Lord and help their brethren for a time; but when their appointed job is finished, they head for home to do what they want to do.

3. The officers encourage their leader (Josh. 1:16-18)
The pronoun "they" probably refers to all the officers Joshua had addressed and not to the leaders of the two and a half tribes alone. What an encouragement they were to their new leader!

To begin with, they encouraged him *by assuring him of their complete obedience (vv. 16-17a).* "Command us and we will obey! Send us and we will go!" These officers had no hidden agendas, and they asked for no concessions. They would obey *all* his commands and go *wherever* he would send them. We could use that kind of commitment in the church today! Too many times we are like the men described in Luke 9:57-62, each of whom put something personal ahead of following the Lord.

In his novel *The Marquis of Lossie,* author George MacDonald has one of the characters say, "I find the doing of the will of God leaves me no time for disputing about His plan." That's the attitude Joshua's officers displayed. They were not so attached to Moses that they put him above Joshua. God had appointed both Moses and Joshua, and to disobey the servant was to disobey the Master. Joshua didn't have to explain or defend his orders. He simply had to give the orders, and the men would obey them.

The officers encouraged Joshua *by praying for him (v. 17).* "The Lord thy God be with thee, as he was with Moses." The best thing we can do for those who lead us is to pray for them daily and ask God to be with them. Joshua was a trained man with vast experience, but that was no guarantee of success. *No Christian worker succeeds to the glory of God apart from prayer.* "Is prayer your steering wheel or your spare tire?" asked Corrie Ten Boom, a question that especially applies to those in places of leadership. When Joshua did not pause to seek the mind of God, he failed miserably (Josh. 7 and 9); and so will we.

They encouraged Joshua by *assuring him that their obedience was a matter of life or death (1:18).* They took his leadership and their responsibilities seriously. Later, Achan didn't take Joshua's orders seriously, and he was killed (Acts 7:15). "But why do you call Me 'Lord, Lord,' and not do the things which I say?" (Luke 6:46, NKJV) If God's people today saw obedience to Christ a matter of life or death, it would make a big difference in our ministry to a lost world. We obey the Lord's orders if we feel like it, if it's convenient, and if we can get something out of it. With soldiers like that, Joshua would never have conquered the Promised Land!

Finally, they encouraged him by *reminding him of the Word of God (v. 18b)*. Moses told Joshua to "be ye of good courage" when he sent him and the other men into Canaan to spy out the land (Num. 13:20). Moses repeated the words when he installed Joshua as his successor (Deut. 31:7, 23). These words were written in the Book of the Law, and Joshua was commanded to read that Book and meditate on it day and night (Josh. 1:8).

Four times in this chapter you find the words "be strong and of good courage" (vv. 6-7, 9, 18). *If we are to conquer the enemy and claim our inheritance in Christ, we must have spiritual strength and spiritual courage.* "Be strong in the Lord, and in the power of His might" (Eph. 6:10).

> Soldiers of Christ, arise,
> And put your armor on,
> Strong in the strength which God supplies
> Of His eternal Son.
>
> [Charles Wesley]

The first step toward winning the battle and claiming our inheritance is to let God encourage us and then for us to encourage others. A discouraged army is never victorious.

"See, the Lord your God has given you the land. Go up and take possession of it as the Lord, the God of your fathers, told you. Do not be afraid; do not be discouraged" (Deut. 1:21, NIV).

Be strong! The battle is the Lord's!

A Convert in Canaan

Only two women are personally named in Hebrews 11, "The Hall of Fame of Faith": *Sarah,* the wife of Abraham (v. 11), and *Rahab,* the harlot of Jericho (v. 31).

Sarah was a godly woman, the wife of the founder of the Hebrew race; and God used her dedicated body to bring Isaac into the world. But Rahab was an ungodly Gentile who worshiped pagan gods and sold her body for money. Humanly speaking, Sarah and Rahab had nothing in common. But from the *divine* viewpoint, Sarah and Rahab shared the most important thing in life: *They both had exercised saving faith in the true and living God.*

Not only does the Bible associate Rahab with Sarah; but in James 2:21-26, it also associates her with *Abraham.* James used both Abraham and Rahab to illustrate the fact that true saving faith always proves itself by good works.

But there's more: The Bible associates Rahab with the Messiah! When you read the genealogy of the Lord Jesus Christ in Matthew 1, you find Rahab's name listed there (v. 5), along with Jacob, David, and the other famous people in the messianic line. She has certainly come a long way from being a pagan prostitute to being an ancestress of the Messiah! "But where sin abounded, grace did much more abound" (Rom. 5:20).

But keep in mind that the most important thing about Rahab was her faith. That's the most important thing about any person, for "without faith it is impossible to please Him [God]" (Heb. 11:6). Not everything that is called "faith" is really true faith, the kind of faith that is described in the Bible. What kind of faith did Rahab have?

1. Courageous faith (Josh. 2:1-7)

Both Hebrews 11:31 and James 2:25 indicate that Rahab had put her faith in Jehovah God *before* the spies ever arrived in Jericho. Like the people in Thessalonica, she had "turned to God from idols to serve the living and true God" (1 Thes. 1:9). She wasn't like the people of Samaria centuries later who "feared the Lord, and [at the same time] served their own gods" (2 Kings 17:33).

Jericho was one of many "city-states" in Canaan, each one ruled by a king (see Josh. 12:9-24). The city covered about eight or nine acres, and there is archeological evidence that double walls about fifteen feet apart protected the city. Rahab's house was on the wall (2:15).

Meanwhile, Jericho was a strategic city in Joshua's plan for conquering Canaan. After taking Jericho, Joshua could then cut straight across and divide the land; and then it would be much easier to defeat the cities in the south and then in the north.

Forty years before, Moses had sent twelve spies into Canaan; and only two of them had given an encouraging report (Num. 13). Joshua sent two men to spy out the land and especially to get information about Jericho. Joshua wanted to know how the citizens were reacting to the arrival of the people of Israel. Since Joshua knew that God had already given him the land and the people, the sending of the spies wasn't an act of unbelief (see 1:11, 15). A good general wants to learn all he can about the enemy before he goes into battle.

How did the two spies make their way through the city without being immediately recognized as strangers? How did they meet Rahab? We certainly have to believe in the providence of God as we watch this drama taking place. Rahab was the only person in Jericho who trusted the God of Israel, and God brought the spies to her.

The Hebrew word translated "harlot" can also mean "one who keeps an inn." If all we had was the Old Testament text, we could absolve Rahab of immorality and call her the "proprietress of an inn." But there is no escape, for in James 2:25 and Hebrews 11:31, the writers use the Greek word that definitely means "a prostitute."

It's remarkable how God in His grace uses people we might think could never become His servants. "But God has chosen the foolish things of the world to put to shame the wise, and God has chosen the weak things of the world to put to shame the things which are mighty; and the base things of the world and the things which are despised God has chosen, and the things which are not, to bring to nothing the things that are, that no flesh should glory in His presence" (1 Cor. 1:27-29, NKJV). Jesus was the "friend of publicans and sinners" (Luke 7:34), and He wasn't ashamed to have a former prostitute in His family tree!

Rahab took her life in her hands when she welcomed the spies and hid them, but that in itself was evidence of her faith in the Lord. *True saving faith can't be hidden for long.* Since these two men represented God's people, she was not afraid to assist them in their cause. Had the king discovered her deception, he would have slain her as a traitor.

Since Rahab was a believer at that time, how do we defend her lies? On the one hand, she demonstrated her faith in the Lord by risking her life to protect the spies; but, on the other hand, she acted like any pagan in the city when she lied about her guests. Perhaps we're expecting too much from a new believer whose knowledge of God was adequate for salvation but certainly limited when it came to the practical things of life. If seasoned believers like Abraham and Isaac resorted to deception (Gen. 12:10-20; 20; 26:6-11), as well as David (1 Sam. 21:2), we had better not be too hard on Rahab. This is not to excuse or encourage lying, but simply to take her circumstances into consideration lest we condemn her too severely.

Lying is wrong (Prov. 12:22), and the fact that God had Rahab's lies recorded in Scripture is no proof that He approved of them. However, let's confess that most of us would hesitate to tell the truth *if it really were a matter of life or death.* It's one thing for *me* to tell the truth about myself and suffer for it; but do I have the right to cause the death of *others,* especially those who have come under my roof for protection? Many people have been honored for deceiving the enemy *during wartime* and saving innocent lives, and this was war! Suppose we looked upon Rahab as a "freedom fighter"; would that change the picture at all?

Ethical problems aside, the main lesson here is that Rahab's faith was conspicuous, and she demonstrated it by receiving the spies and risking her life to protect them. James saw her actions as proof that she was truly a believer (James 2:25). Her faith wasn't hidden; the spies could tell that she was indeed a believer.

2. Confident faith (Josh. 2:8-11)
Faith is only as good as its object. Some people have faith in faith and think that just by *believing* they can make great things happen. Others have faith in lies, which is not faith at all but superstition. I once heard a psychologist say that the people in a support group "must have some kind of faith,

even if it's faith in the soft drink machine." But faith is only as good as its object. How much help can you get from a soft drink machine, especially after you've run out of money?

D. Martyn Lloyd-Jones reminds us that "faith shows itself in the whole personality." True saving faith isn't just a feat of intellectual gymnastics by which we convince ourselves that something is true that really isn't true. Nor is it merely a stirring of the emotions that gives us a false sense of confidence that God will do what we *feel* He will do. Nor is it a courageous act of the will whereby we jump off the pinnacle of the temple and expect God to rescue us (Matt. 4:5-7). True saving faith involves "the whole personality": the mind is instructed, the emotions are stirred, and the will then acts in obedience to God.

"By faith Noah, being warned of God of things not seen as yet [the intellect], moved with fear [the emotions], prepared an ark [the will] . . ." (Heb. 11:7). Rahab's experience was similar to that of Noah: *She knew* that Jehovah was the true God [the mind]; *she feared* for herself and her family when she heard about the great wonders He had performed [the emotions]; and *she received* the spies and pleaded for the salvation of her family [the will]. Unless the whole personality is involved, it is not saving faith as the Bible describes it.

Of course, this doesn't mean that the mind must be fully instructed in every aspect of Bible truth before a sinner can be saved. The woman with the hemorrhage only touched the hem of Christ's garment and she was healed, but she acted on the little knowledge that she did possess (Matt. 9:20-22). Rahab's knowledge of the true God was meager, but she acted on what she knew; and the Lord saved her.

Rahab showed more faith in the Lord than the ten spies had exhibited forty years before, when she said, "I know that the Lord has given you the land" (Josh. 2:9, NKJV). Her faith was based on facts, not just feelings; for she had heard of the miracles God had performed, starting with the opening up of the Red Sea at the Exodus. "So then faith comes by hearing, and hearing by the Word of God" (Rom. 10:17, NKJV).

Since the report of the Lord's power had traveled to the people of Canaan, they were afraid; but this is what Israel expected their great God to do. "The people shall hear, and be afraid: sorrow shall take hold on the inhabitants of Palestina. Then the dukes of Edom shall be amazed; the mighty men of Moab, trembling shall take hold upon them; all the inhabitants of Canaan shall melt away. Fear and dread shall fall upon them" (Ex. 15:14-16). God promised to do this for Israel, and He kept His promise. "This day I will begin to put the dread and fear of you upon the nations under the whole heaven, who shall hear the report of you, and shall tremble and be in anguish because of you" (Deut. 2:25, NKJV).

"The Lord your God, He is God in heaven above, and in earth beneath" (Josh. 2:11). What a confession of faith from the lips of a woman whose life had been imprisoned in pagan idolatry! She believed in *one God,* not in the multitude of gods that populated the heathen temples. She believed He was a *personal* God ("your God"), who would work on behalf of those who trusted Him. She believed He was *the God of Israel,* who would give the land to His people. This God whom she trusted was not limited to one nation or one land, but was *the God of heaven and earth.* Rahab believed in a great and awesome God!

Our confidence that we are God's children comes from the witness of the Word of God before us and the witness of the Spirit of God within us (1 John 5:9-13). However, the assurance of salvation isn't based only on what we know from the Bible or how we feel in our hearts. It's also based on how we live; for if there hasn't been a change in our behavior, then it's doubtful that we've truly been born again (2 Cor. 5:21; James 2:14-26). It isn't enough to say "Lord, Lord!" We must obey what He tells us to do (Matt. 7:21-27). Rahab's obedience gave evidence of a changed life.

Rahab's conversion was truly an act of God's grace. Like all the citizens of Canaan, Rahab was under condemnation and destined to die. God commanded the Jews to "utterly destroy them" and show them no mercy (Deut. 7:1-3). Rahab was a Gentile, outside the covenant mercies shown to Israel (Eph. 2:11-13). She didn't deserve to be saved, but God had mercy on her. If ever a sinner experienced Ephesians 2:1-10, it was Rahab!

3. Concerned faith (Josh. 2:12-14)

Rahab, however, wasn't concerned only about her own welfare, for once she had personally experienced the grace and mercy of God, she was burdened to rescue her family. After Andrew met the Lord Jesus, he shared the good news with his brother Simon and brought him to Jesus (John 1:35-42). The cleansed leper went home and told everybody he met what Jesus had done for him (Mark 1:40-45). "The fruit of the righteous is a tree of life; and he that winneth souls is wise" (Prov. 11:30).

Rahab wanted assurance from the two spies that when the city was taken, they would guarantee her family's safety. The men gave her that guarantee in two ways: They pledged their word, and they pledged their lives that they would not break their word. In other words, they became surety for Rahab's family, the way Judah became surety for Benjamin (Gen. 43:8-9). The Book of Proverbs warns against *"suretyship"* in the business world because it involves a risk that could lead to your losing everything (Prov. 6:1ff; 11:15; 20:16; 27:13). However, in the realm of the spiritual, we are saved because Jesus Christ, who owed no debts, was willing to become surety for us (Heb. 7:22, NIV). The next time you sing "Jesus Paid It All," remember that Jesus has pledged Himself as "the guarantee of a better covenant" (Heb. 7:22, NIV). He died for us; and as long as He lives, our salvation is secure. Because of the promise of His Word and the guarantee of His eternal suretyship, we have confidence that "He is able to save completely [forever] those who come to God through Him, because He always lives to intercede for them" (v. 25, NIV).

The spies warned Rahab that she must not divulge any of this information to anybody in the city other than the members of her family. If she did, their agreement was canceled. What a contrast to the believer's relationship to Jesus Christ, for He wants *everybody* to know that He has paid the price of redemption and that they can be saved by trusting Him. If Rahab talked too much, her life was in danger; but if we don't talk enough, the lives of lost people around us are in danger.

4. Covenant faith (Josh. 2:15-24)

A covenant is simply an agreement, a contract between two or more parties, with certain conditions laid down for all parties to obey. You find a number of *divine* covenants recorded in Scripture: God's covenant with our first parents in Eden (Gen. 2:16); God's covenants with Noah (Gen. 9), Abraham (12:1-3; 15:1-20), and Israel (Ex. 19-20); the covenant concerning the land of Palestine, as explained in Deuteronomy; the messianic covenant with David (2 Sam. 7); and the New Covenant in the blood of Jesus Christ (Jer. 31:31; Matt. 26:28; Heb. 12:24). You also find *human* covenants, such as the agreement between David and Jonathan (1 Sam. 18:3; 20:16) and between David and the people of Israel (2 Sam. 5:1-5).

Before the two spies left Rahab's house, they reaffirmed their covenant with her. Since the men didn't know God's plan for taking the city, they couldn't give Rahab any detailed instructions. Perhaps they assumed that the city would be besieged, the gates smashed down, and the people massacred. The men were certain that the city would fall and that ultimately the land would be taken.

Often in biblical covenants, God appointed some physical or material "token" to remind the people of what had been promised. His covenant with Abraham was "sealed" by the rite of circumcision (Gen. 17:9-14; Rom. 4:11). When God established His covenant with Israel at Sinai, both the covenant book and the covenant people were sprinkled with blood (Ex. 24:3-8; Heb. 9:16-22). God gave the rainbow as the token of the covenant with Noah (Gen. 9:12-17), and the Lord Jesus Christ used the broken bread and the cup of wine as tokens of the New Covenant (Luke 22:19-20; 1 Cor. 11:23-26).

In the case of Rahab, the spies instructed her to hang a scarlet rope out of the window of her house, which was built into the wall (Josh. 2:18). This scarlet rope would identify the "house of safety" to the army of Israel when they came to take the city. The color of the rope is significant for it reminds us of blood. Just as the blood on the doorposts in Egypt marked a house that the angel of death was to pass over (Ex. 12:1-13), so the scarlet rope marked a house on the Jericho wall whose occupants the Jewish soldiers were to protect. Rahab let the men down from the window with that rope and kept it in the window from that hour. This was the "sure sign" of the covenant that she had asked for (Josh. 2:12-23).

It's important to note that Rahab and her family were saved by faith in the God of Israel and not by faith in the rope hanging out the window. The fact that she hung the rope from the window was proof that she had faith, just as the blood of the slain lamb put on the doorposts in Egypt proved that the Jews believed God's Word. Faith in the living God means salvation, and faith in His covenant gives assurance; but faith in *the token of the covenant* is religious superstition and can give neither salvation nor assurance. The Jews depended on circumcision to save them, but they ignored the true spiritual meaning of that important rite (Rom. 2:25-29; Deut. 10:12-16; 30:6). Many people today depend for their salvation on their baptism or their participation in the Lord's Table (the Eucharist, Communion); but this kind of faith is vain. Rahab had faith in the Lord and in the covenant promises He had made through His servants; and she proved her faith by hanging the scarlet rope from the window. When the Jews captured Jericho, they found Rahab and her family in her house; and they rescued them from judgment (Josh. 6:21-25).

Rahab was a woman of great courage. She had to tell all her relatives about the coming judgment and the promise of salvation, and this was a dangerous thing to do. Suppose one of those relatives told the king what was going on. She also had to give a reason for the scarlet line hanging out her window. Since Jericho was "securely shut up" (v. 1, NKJV), it isn't likely that there were people outside the walls; but a stranger coming into the city for safety might have seen the scarlet cord. Or somebody visiting Rahab's house might have asked about it.

The spies left Rahab's house and hid until they were sure their pursuers had given up the chase. Then they returned to the camp of Israel and gave Joshua the good news that the fear of the Lord had brought the people of the land to a place of helplessness. Rahab not only brought hope to her family, but she also gave great encouragement to Joshua and the army of Israel.

The people of Israel, however, weren't ready yet to cross the river and conquer the enemy. They had some "unfinished business" to take care of before they could be sure of the blessing of the Lord.

F O U R

Forward by Faith

We've just examined the faith of an individual, Rahab; and now the focus in the Book of Joshua moves to the faith of an entire nation. As you study, keep in mind that this book deals with much more than ancient history — what God did centuries ago for the Jews. It's about your life and the life of the church today — what God wants to do here and now for those who trust Him. The Book of Joshua is about the victory of faith and the glory that comes to God when His people trust and obey. British Prime Minister Benjamin Disraeli said, "The world was never conquered by intrigue; it was conquered by faith."

In the Christian life you're either an *overcomer* or you're *overcome,* a victor or a victim. After all, God didn't save us to make statues out of us and put us on exhibition. He saved us to make soldiers out of us and move us forward by faith to claim our rich inheritance in Jesus Christ. Moses said it perfectly: "He brought us out... that He might bring us in" (Deut. 6:23). Too many of God's people have the mistaken idea that salvation — being delivered from the bondage of Egypt — is all that's involved in the Christian life; but salvation is only the beginning. Both in our personal spiritual

44

growth and in our service for the Lord, "there remains very much land yet to be possessed" (Josh. 13:1, NKJV). The theme of the Book of Joshua is the theme of the Book of Hebrews: "Let us go on" (Heb. 6:1); and the only way to go on is by faith.

Unbelief says, "Let's go back to where it's safe"; but faith says, "Let's go forward to where God is working" (see Num. 14:1-4). Forty years before, Joshua and Caleb had assured the Jews, "Let us go up at once, and possess it; for we are well able to overcome it." That's faith! But the people said, "We are not able!" That's unbelief, and it cost the nation forty years of discipline in the wilderness (see Num. 13:26-33). "And this is the victory that has overcome the world—your faith" (1 John 5:4, NKJV).

One of the joys of my Christian life has been the study of Christian biography, the lives of the men and women whom God has used—and is using—to challenge the church and change the world. The Christians I've read about were all different in their backgrounds, their training, their personalities, and their ways of serving God; but they had one thing in common: *They all believed God's promises and did what He told them to do.* They were men and women of faith, and God honored them because they believed His Word.

God hasn't changed, and the principle of faith hasn't changed. What seems to have changed is the attitude of God's people: *We no longer believe God and act by faith in His promises.* His promises never fail (Josh. 21:45; 23:14; 1 Kings 8:56), but we can fail to live by the grace of God and not enter into all that He has promised for us (Heb. 3:7-19; 12:15). God has "brought us out that He might bring us in," but too often we fail to "enter in because of unbelief" (Heb. 3:19).

In Joshua 3 and 4, God illustrates for us three essentials for moving ahead by faith and claiming all that He has for us: the Word of faith, the walk of faith, and the witness of faith.

45

1. The Word of faith (Josh. 3:1-13)

As the nation waited by the Jordan River, the people must have wondered what Joshua planned to do. He certainly wouldn't ask them to swim the river or ford it, because the river was at flood stage (3:15). They couldn't construct enough boats or rafts to transport more than a million people over the water to the other side. Besides, that approach would make them perfect targets for their enemies. What would their new leader do?

Like Moses before him, Joshua received his orders from the Lord, and he obeyed them by faith. "So then faith comes by hearing, and hearing by the word of God" (Rom. 10:17, NKJV). It has been well said that faith is not believing in spite of evidence but obeying in spite of consequence. When you read Hebrews 11, the great "faith chapter" of Scripture, you discover that the people mentioned there all *did something* because they believed God. Their faith wasn't a passive feeling; it was an active force. Because Abraham believed God, he left Ur and headed for Canaan. Because Moses believed God, he defied the gods of Egypt and led the Jews to freedom. Because Gideon believed God, he led a small band of Jews to defeat the huge Midianite army. *Living faith always leads to action.* "For as the body without the spirit is dead, so faith without works is dead also" (James 2:26, NKJV).

In this paragraph, you find five different messages, all of them based on the Word of God, which is the "word of faith" (Rom. 10:8). The people obeyed these messages by faith, and God took them over the river.

The officers' message to the people (vv. 1-4). Joshua was an early riser (6:12; 7:16; 8:10), who spent the first hours of the day in communion with God (1:8). In this, he was like Moses (Ex. 24:4; 34:4), David (Ps. 57:8; see 119:147), Hezekiah (2 Chron. 29:20), and our Lord Jesus Christ (Mark 1:35; see Isa. 50:4). It's impossible to live by faith and ignore the Word of

God and prayer (Acts 6:4); for faith is nurtured by worship and the Word. The people God uses and blesses know how to discipline their bodies so that they can give themselves to the Lord in the early morning hours.

Joshua ordered the camp to move ten miles from The Acacia Grove (Shittim) to the Jordan; and no doubt the people in Jericho watched this march with great apprehension. It probably took Israel a day to make this journey; they rested another day; and on the third day, the officers gave them their orders: The people were to cross the river, following the ark of the covenant.

The ark is mentioned sixteen times in chapters 3 and 4. It's called "the ark of the covenant" ten times, "the ark of the Lord" three times, and simply "the ark" three times. It was the "throne of God," the place where His glory rested in the tabernacle (Ex. 25:10-22) and God sat "enthroned between the cherubim" (Ps. 80:1, NIV). The Law of God was kept in the ark, a reminder of God's covenant with Israel; and the blood of the sacrifices was sprinkled on the mercy seat on the annual Day of Atonement (Lev. 16:14-15).

The ark going before the people was an encouragement to their faith, for it meant that their God was going before them and opening up the way. God had promised Moses, "My Presence will go with you, and I will give you rest" (Ex. 33:14, NKJV). When the nation had marched through the wilderness, the ark had gone before them (Num. 10:33); and Moses would say, "Rise up, O Lord! May Your enemies be scattered; may Your foes flee before You" (v. 35, NIV). On that occasion, the presence of the ark was a guarantee of the presence of the Lord.

Each of the tribes had an assigned place in the camp and an assigned order in the march when they broke up camp (Josh. 2). When the leaders of the tribes saw the priests bearing the ark and moving toward the river, they were to prepare their people to follow. Since the people had not traveled this way before, they needed God to guide them. But they were not to get too close to the ark, for this was a holy piece of furniture from the tabernacle; and it was not to be treated carelessly. God is our companion as we go through life, but we dare not treat Him like a "buddy."

Joshua's message to the people (v. 5). This was both an order and a promise, and the fulfillment of the promise depended on their obedience to the order. Some of God's promises are unconditional, and all we have to do is believe them; while other promises require that we meet certain conditions. In meeting these conditions, we're not earning God's blessing; we're making sure our hearts are ready for God's blessing.

If the experience of Israel at Mt. Sinai was the pattern (Ex. 19:9-15), "sanctify yourselves" meant that everybody bathed and changed their clothes and that the married couples devoted themselves wholly to the Lord (1 Cor. 7:1-6). In the Near East, however, water was a luxury that wasn't used too often for personal hygiene. In our modern world we're accustomed to comfortable bathing facilities; but these were unknown to most of the people in Bible times.

In the Bible the imagery of washing one's body and changing clothes symbolized making a new beginning with the Lord. Since sin is pictured as defilement (Ps. 51:2, 7), God has to cleanse us before we can truly follow Him. When Jacob made a new beginning with the Lord and returned to Bethel, he and his family washed themselves and changed their garments (Gen. 35:1-3). After King David confessed his sin, he bathed, changed clothes, and worshiped the Lord (2 Sam. 12:20). The imagery is carried over into the New Testament in 2 Corinthians 6:14–7:1; Ephesians 4:26-27, and Colossians 3:8-14.

The promise was that the Lord would do wonders among them. As He opened the Red Sea to deliver Israel from

Egypt, so also He would open the Jordan River and take them into the Promised Land. But that would be just the beginning of miracles, for the Lord would go with them into the land, defeat their enemies, and enable the tribes to claim their inheritance. "Who is so great a God as our God? You are the God who does wonders" (Ps. 77:13-14, NKJV). "How great are His signs, And how mighty His wonders!" (Dan. 4:3, NKJV)

Joshua's message to the priests (v. 6). The priests had the responsibility of bearing the ark of the covenant and going before the people as they marched. It was the priests who had to get their feet wet before God would open the waters. The priests would also have to stand in the middle of the riverbed until all the people had passed over. When the priests arrived on the other side, the waters would return to their original condition. It took faith and courage for these priests to do their job, but they trusted God and relied on the faithfulness of His Word.

The message of the Lord to Joshua (vv. 7-8). When Moses led the nation through the Red Sea, this miracle magnified Moses before the people; and they recognized that he was indeed the servant of the Lord (Ex. 14:31). God would do the same thing for Joshua at the Jordan; and in so doing, He would remind the people that He was with Joshua just as He had been with Moses (Josh. 4:14; see 1:5, 9). Both Moses and Joshua had received their *authority* from the Lord before these miracles occurred, but the miracles gave them *stature* before the people. It takes both authority and stature to exercise effective leadership.

Joshua's message to the people (vv. 9-13). Having instructed the priests bearing the ark, Joshua then shared the words of the Lord with the people. He didn't magnify himself; He magnified the Lord and His gracious blessings to the nation. True spiritual leadership focuses the eyes of God's people on the Lord and His greatness. Much of what Joshua said in this brief speech was recalled from Moses' last speech to Joshua (Deut. 31:1-8), as well as the Lord's words to Joshua when he took Moses' place (Josh. 1:1-9). Joshua didn't give the people a "religious pep talk." He simply reminded them of the promises of God—the Word of faith—and encouraged them to trust and obey.

But Joshua's God was more than just the God of Israel. He was "the living God" (3:10) and "the Lord of all the earth" (vv. 11, 13). Because He is "the living God," He can defeat the dead idols of the heathen nations that then inhabited the land (Ps. 115). Because He is "the Lord of all the earth," He can go where He pleases and do what He wishes with every land and nation. "You shall be a special treasure to Me above all people," God had told them at Sinai, "for all the earth is Mine" (Ex. 19:5, NKJV). "The hills melted like wax at the presence of the Lord, at the presence of the Lord of the whole earth" (Ps. 97:5).

Joshua explained to the people that God would open the river as soon as the priests bearing the ark put their feet into the waters of the Jordan. He also ordered each tribe to appoint a man to perform a special task that was explained later (Josh. 4:2-8). God was going before His people, and He would open the way!

As you review these five messages, you can see that the Lord gave them all the information they needed to accomplish what He wanted them to do. You find conditions that the people had to fulfill, orders they had to obey, and promises they had to believe. God always gives His "Word of faith" to His people whenever He asks them to follow Him into new areas of conflict and conquest. God's commandments are still His enablements, and God's promises do not fail. The counsel of King Jehoshaphat centuries later is still applicable today: "Believe in the Lord your God, and you shall be established; believe His prophets, and you shall prosper" (2 Chron. 20:20, NKJV). "There has not failed one word of all His good promise" (1 Kings 8:56, NKJV).

2. The walk of faith (Josh. 3:14-17)

During most of the year, the Jordan River was about a hundred feet wide; but at the spring flood season, the river overflowed its banks and became a mile wide. As soon as the priests bearing the ark put their feet into the river, the water stopped flowing and stood like a wall about twenty miles away upstream, near a city called Adam. It was a miracle of God in response to the faith of the people.

Unless we step out by faith (1:3) and "get our feet wet," we're not likely to make much progress in living for Christ and serving Him. Each step that the priests took opened the water before them until they were standing in the midst of the river on dry ground. They stood there as the people passed by; and when the whole nation had crossed, the priests walked to the shore and the flow of the water resumed.

When God opened the Red Sea, He used a strong wind that blew the whole night before (Ex. 14:21-22). This was not an accident, for the wind was the blast of God's nostrils (15:8). When Moses lifted his rod, the wind began to blow; and when he lowered the rod, the waters flowed back and drowned the Egyptian army (14:26-28). When Israel crossed the Jordan River, it was not the obedient arm of a leader that brought the miracle but the obedient feet of the people. Unless we are willing to step out by faith and obey His Word, God can never open the way for us.

As I mentioned before, the crossing of the Jordan River is not a picture of the Christian dying and going to heaven, contrary to what is said in some songs. The crossing of the Red Sea pictures the believer being delivered from the bondage of sin, and the crossing of the Jordan River pictures the believer claiming the inheritance in Jesus Christ. Joshua is a type of Jesus Christ our Conqueror who leads us from day to day into the inheritance He has planned for us (1 Cor. 2:9-10). "He shall choose our inheritance for us" (Ps. 47:4).

What a tragedy it is when God's people fail to claim their inheritance and wander aimlessly through life as Israel did in the wilderness. The Book of Hebrews was written to challenge God's people to go on in spiritual maturity and not go backward in unbelief. In Hebrews 3–4, the writer used Israel's experience at Kadesh Barnea to warn foolish Christians not to come short of all that God had planned for them. We never stand still in the Christian life; we either move forward in faith or go backward in unbelief.

3. The witness of faith (Josh. 4:1-24)
The Lord was in control of all the activities at the Jordan River that day. He told the priests when to enter the river and when to leave and go to the other side. He told the water when to roll back and when to return. Both the water and the people obeyed Him, and everything worked out as God planned. It was a day that glorified the Lord and magnified His servant Joshua (v. 14).

Two heaps of stones were set up as memorials of Israel's crossing of the Jordan River: twelve stones at Gilgal (vv. 1-8, 10-24), and twelve stones in the midst of the river (v. 9). They were witnesses that God honors faith and works on behalf of those who trust Him.

The stones placed at Gilgal were carried over by twelve previously selected men, one from each tribe (3:12). When these men reached the midst of the river, they each picked up a large stone and carried it about eight miles to Gilgal where the nation camped for the night. Gilgal was about two miles from Jericho and excluding the transjordan was the first territory in Canaan claimed by Israel for their inheritance. In later years Gilgal became an important center for the nation. Israel crowned their first king at Gilgal (1 Sam. 11); there David was welcomed back after Absalom's rebellion was subdued (2 Sam. 19); and Samuel thought Gilgal important enough to include it in his "ministry circuit" (1 Sam. 7:16). There was a "school of the prophets" at Gilgal in the days of Elijah and Elisha (2 Kings 2:1-2; 4:38). Gilgal was important to Joshua because it became his camp and center of operations (Josh. 9:6; 10:6, 15, 43; 14:6).

This heap of twelve stones was a reminder of what God did for His people. The Jews were great believers in teaching the next generation about Jehovah and His special relationship to the people of Israel (4:6, 21; Ex. 12:26; 13:14; Deut. 6:20; see Pss. 34:11-16; 71:17-18; 78:1-7; 79:13; 89:1; 102:18). To an unbeliever, the heap of twelve stones was simply another stone pile; but to a believing Israelite, it was a constant reminder that Jehovah was his or her God, working His wonders on behalf of His people.

But also note that Joshua put an obligation on the Jews to fear the Lord and bear witness of Him to the whole world (Josh. 4:24). The God who can open the river is the God everybody ought to fear, love, and obey! Israel needed to tell the other nations about Him and invite them to trust Him too. The God of Israel cares for His people, keeps His promises, goes before them in victory, and never fails. What a witness to give to the world!

It's unfortunate that this memorial at Gilgal gradually lost its spiritual meaning and instead became a shrine where the Jews sinned against God by worshiping there. The Prophet Hosea condemned the people for worshiping at Gilgal instead of at Jerusalem (Hosea 4:15; 9:15; 12:11), and Amos echoed his warnings (Amos 4:4; 5:5). Unless we teach the next generation the truth about the Lord, they will turn away and start following the world.

Joshua set up the monument in the midst of the river (v. 9)*; and to the Jews, it must have seemed a strange thing for their leader to do. After all, who but God could see twelve stones heaped together in a riverbed? We aren't told that God commanded Joshua to set up this second monument, but it's likely that He did. At least, He didn't reproach him for doing it.

The monument at Gilgal reminded the Jews that God had opened the Jordan River and brought them safely across into the Promised Land. They had made a break with the past and were never to think of going back. The monument in the depths of the river reminded them that their old life was buried and they were now to "walk in newness of life" (Rom. 6:1-4). (When we study Josh. 5, we will see the spiritual significance for the Christian today of the establishing of this monument and the circumcising of the new generation.)

Meanwhile, whenever the Jewish children asked about the twelve stones at Gilgal, the parents would explain the miracle of the crossing of the river. Then they would add, "But there's another monument in the middle of the river where the priests stood with the ark. You can't see it, but it's there. It reminds us that our old life has been buried, and we must live a new life in obedience to the Lord." The children would have to accept this fact by faith; and if they did, it could make a great difference in the way they related to God and to His will for their lives.

These two heaps of stones were the first of several stone monuments that the Jews put up in the land. In obedience to Moses' instructions, they also set up the two "stones of

---

*The NIV text applies the verse to the monument at Gilgal, but the marginal note makes this a separate monument, which I think is the accurate interpretation. The NASB reads, "Then Joshua set up twelve stones in the middle of the Jordan at the place where the feet of the priests who carried the ark of the covenant were standing, and they are there to this day."

blessing and cursing" at Mt. Ebal and Mt. Gerizim (Deut. 27:1-8; Josh. 8:30-35). They raised a heap of stones over Achan and his household (7:25-26); and at the close of his life, Joshua set up a "witness stone" at Shechem (24:24-28; Jud. 9:6). The two and a half tribes that lived east of the Jordan set up a "great altar" to remind their children that they were a part of the nation of Israel, even though the river separated them from the other tribes (Josh. 22:10ff).

There is nothing wrong with memorials, provided they don't become religious idols that turn our hearts from God, and provided they don't so link us to the past that we fail to serve God in the present. Glorifying the past is a good way to petrify the present and rob the church of power. The next generations need reminders of what God has done in history, but these reminders must also strengthen their faith and draw them closer to the Lord.

God brings us out that He might bring us in (Deut. 6:23), and He brings us in that we might overcome and claim our inheritance in Jesus Christ. Because God's people are identified with Christ in His death, burial, and resurrection (Rom. 6; Gal. 2:20), they have "overcoming power," and the world (6:14), the flesh (5:24), or the devil (John 12:31) need not defeat them. In Jesus Christ, we are overcomers (1 John 5:3).

If you want to claim your spiritual inheritance in Christ, believe the Word of faith and *get your feet wet!* Step out in a walk of faith, and God will open the way for you. Surrender yourself to the Lord and die to the old life (Rom. 6), and He will bring you into the land and give you "days of heaven upon the earth" (Deut. 11:21).

The Israelites were now in the land, but they were not yet ready to confront the enemy. There was still some spiritual preparation necessary for the people and for Joshua.

Preparing for Victory

The nation of Israel arrived safely on the other side of the Jordan River. Their crossing was a great miracle, and it sent a great message to the people of the land (5:1). The Canaanites were already afraid (2:9-11), and now their fears totally demoralized them.

You would have expected Joshua to mobilize the army immediately and attack Jericho. After all, the people of Israel were united in following the Lord; and the people of the land were paralyzed by fear. From the human point of view, it was the perfect time for Joshua to act.

But God's thoughts and ways are higher than ours (Isa. 55:8-9); and Joshua was getting his orders from the Lord, not from the military experts. The nation crossed the river on the tenth day of the first month (Josh. 4:19). The events described in Joshua 5 took at least ten days, and then the people marched around Jericho for six more days. God waited over two weeks before giving His people their first victory in the land.

God's people must be *prepared* before they can be trusted with victory. The triumphant conquest of the land was to be the victory of God, not the victory of Israel or of Joshua. It was neither the expertise of the Jewish army nor the emotions of the enemy that would give Israel the victory, but the presence and blessing of the Lord. There were three steps of preparation necessary before God would give His people victory over the nations in the land of Canaan.

1. Renewing the Lord's covenant (Josh. 5:1-9)

After triumphantly crossing the Jordan River, the nation had to pause at Gilgal while the men submitted to painful surgery. Why did God command this ritual at this time?

To restore their covenant relationship (Josh. 5:2-7). Israel is a *covenant nation,* a privilege God has given to no other nation on earth (Rom. 9:4-5). God gave His covenant to Abraham when He called him out of Ur of the Chaldees (Gen. 12:1-3), and He sealed that covenant with a sacrifice (Gen. 15). God gave circumcision as the *sign* of the covenant to Abraham and his descendants (17:9-14, 23-27; note especially v. 11). Other nations in that day practiced circumcision, but the ritual didn't carry with it the spiritual meaning that it did for the Jews.

Through this ritual the Jews became a "marked people" because they belonged to the true and living God. This meant that they were under obligation to obey Him. The mark of the covenant reminded them that their bodies belonged to the Lord and were not to be used for sinful purposes. Israel was surrounded by nations that worshiped idols and included in their worship rituals that were sensual and degrading. The mark of the covenant reminded the Jews that they were a special people, a separated people, a holy nation (Ex. 19:5-6), and that they were to maintain purity in their marriages, their society, and their worship of God.

The Jews had not practiced circumcision during their years of wandering in the wilderness. Thirty-eight years before, at Kadesh Barnea, they had refused to believe God and enter the land (Deut. 2:14; Num. 13–14). God disciplined the people by making them wander in the wilderness until the entire older generation had died off, except Caleb and Joshua. During that time, God had suspended His covenant relationship with Israel and didn't require the mark of the covenant on their male children. He performed wonders for them and met their every need even though they were temporarily not His covenant people.

The new generation was now in their inheritance, however, and it was important that they renew their covenant relationships with the Lord. If during their wilderness journey Israel was tempted to sin (see Num. 25), how much more they would be tempted now that they were living in the land! They would be surrounded by pagan people with immoral religious practices, and they would be tempted to compromise with their enemies. Later, this is exactly what future generations did, because they forgot the true meaning of circumcision.

This physical operation on the body was meant to be a symbol of *a spiritual operation on the heart.* "Therefore circumcise the foreskin of your heart, and be stiff-necked no longer" (Deut. 10:16, NKJV). No amount of external surgery can change the inner person. It's when we repent and turn to God for help that He can change our hearts and make us love and obey Him more. (See Rom. 2:25-29.)

But over the years, the Jews came to trust in the external *mark* of the covenant and not in the *God* of the covenant who wanted to make them a holy people. They thought that as long as they were God's covenant people, they could live just as they pleased! Moses warned them about this sin (Deut. 30:6), and so did the prophets (Jer. 4:4). When John the Baptist called them to repent, the Jewish spiritual leaders said, "We have Abraham as our father" (Matt. 3:9, NKJV). They were not unlike some people today who feel sure they're saved and are going to heaven because they're baptized, confirmed, and participate regularly in Communion. As good as these religious rites can be, they must never become substitutes for faith in Jesus Christ. (See Rom. 2:25-29.)

To test their faith (Josh 5:8). Israel was camped in enemy territory, just a few miles from Jericho. Now they were going to temporarily disable *every male in the nation,* including every soldier in the army! What a golden opportunity for the enemy to attack and wipe them out. (See Gen. 34.) It took faith for Joshua and the people to obey the Lord, but their obedience to the Law was the secret of their success (Josh. 1:7-8). In their weakness they were made strong; and through faith and patience they inherited the promises (Heb. 6:12).

Shortly after Israel departed from Egypt, God tested them at Meribah; and they failed the test (Ex. 17:1-7; Ps. 81:7). Shortly after Israel entered the Promised Land, God tested them by commanding the men to be circumcised; and they passed the test. The people had faith to obey God, and this act gave evidence that they would obey His orders as they marched through the land.

After we've experienced an exciting victory of faith, God often permits us to be tested. Abraham arrived in the land of promise and was confronted with a famine (Gen. 12). Elijah triumphed over Baal and was threatened with death (1 Kings 18–19). After His baptism in the Jordan, the Spirit led Jesus into the wilderness to be tempted by Satan (Matt. 3:13–4:11). Since great victories can lead to great pride, God allows us to be tested in order to remind us to depend on Him. The Scottish preacher Andrew Bonar (1810–92) used to say, "Let us be as watchful after the victory as before the battle."

To remove their reproach (Josh 5:9). The word *Gilgal* is similar to the Hebrew word *galal* which means "to roll." But what was "the reproach of Egypt"? Some suggest that this means their reproach for being slaves in Egypt, but it wasn't Israel's fault that the new pharaoh turned against them (Ex. 1:8ff). The Jews were in Egypt because God had sent them there (Gen. 46:1-4), not because they were disobedient.

It's also been suggested that "the reproach of Egypt" refers to the nation's shame because they had worshiped idols in Egypt (Ezek. 20:7-8; 23:3) and even during their wilderness wanderings (Amos 5:25-26; Acts 7:42-43). But that older generation was now dead, and the younger Israelites certainly shouldn't be blamed for the sins of their fathers. Furthermore, it's difficult for me to see the relationship between crossing the river, circumcision, and the Jews' idolatry in Egypt.

I think that "the reproach of Egypt" refers to the ridicule of the enemy when Israel failed to trust God at Kadesh Barnea and enter the Promised Land. When Aaron made the golden calf at Mt. Sinai and the people broke God's law, God threatened to destroy them and make a new nation from Moses. But Moses argued that God would lose glory if He did that, because the Egyptians would only say that God delivered them in order to kill them (Ex. 32:1-12). At Kadesh Barnea Moses used the same appeal when God said He would destroy Israel (Num. 14:11-14). Moses didn't want the Egyptians to spread the word that the God of Israel couldn't finish what He had started.

Israel's sin at Kadesh Barnea was a reproach to them, but now that was all in the past. The nation was actually in the Promised Land! They had captured the territory east of the Jordan, and their people were already occupying it (Num. 32). They had crossed the Jordan River and were ready for conquest. No matter what the Egyptians and the other nations had said about Israel because of their sin at Kadesh Barnea, that reproach was now completely gone. Each man bore on his body the mark that reminded him that he belonged to

God, he was a son of the covenant, and the land was his to conquer and possess.

To qualify them to eat the Passover (Ex. 12:43-44, 48). No male could participate in the annual Feast of the Passover unless he had been circumcised and was a true son of the covenant. I'll have more to say later about this great Passover celebration.

To picture some important spiritual truths. Old Testament events are often illustrations of New Testament doctrines (Rom. 15:4; 1 Cor. 10:11). Israel's exodus from Egypt pictures the sinner's deliverance from the slavery of sin through faith in Jesus Christ (John 1:29; 1 Cor. 5:7; Gal. 1:4). Israel's crossing of the Jordan River is a picture of believers dying to self and entering by faith into their inheritance. This truth is explained in Hebrews 1–6, especially chapters 3 and 4. God doesn't want us to wander in the wilderness of unbelief. He wants us to claim our inheritance by faith, conquer our enemies, and enjoy the spiritual "rest" that He has for those who walk by faith.

Because the Holy Spirit baptizes all believers into the body of Christ (1 Cor. 12:13), all believers are identified with Christ in His death, burial, resurrection, and ascension (Rom. 6:1-10; Eph. 2:1-10). This truth is pictured in Israel's crossing of the river. We're saved from the *penalty* of sin because of *substitution:* Christ died for us (Rom. 5:8). But we're saved from the *power* of sin because of *identification:* We died with Christ (Gal. 2:20). We must believe what God says is true and reckon ourselves to be dead to sin and alive in Christ (Rom. 6:11-23). We have crossed the river!

Many New Testament scholars believe the apostolic church practiced baptism by immersion. The candidate was submerged into the water and then raised up, picturing the believer's identification with Christ in His death, burial, and resurrection. Israel pictured this truth in their crossing of the

Red Sea (separated from the old life) and their crossing of the Jordan River (entering into the new inheritance).

We have also been identified with Christ in His circumcision. "In Him you were also circumcised with the circumcision made without hands, by putting off the body of the sins of the flesh, by the circumcision of Christ, buried with Him in baptism, in which you also were raised with Him through faith in the working of God, who raised Him from the dead" (Col. 2:11-12, NKJV).

The Christian's *circumcision* is in contrast to that of the Jews. They had external physical surgery, while believers have internal "spiritual surgery" on their hearts. The Jews' surgery involved only a part of the body; while for the believer, the whole "body of the sins of the flesh" (Col. 2:11) was removed. *When you accept this fact and reckon on it, you have victory over sins of the flesh that would enslave you.* Faith "in the working of God" (Col. 2:12, NKJV) can give you overcoming power.

In the early church there were false teachers who said the Gentile Christians had to be circumcised and obey the Law of Moses, or they couldn't be saved (Acts 15). They were adding human works to God's grace (Eph. 2:8-10; Gal. 5:1). Paul called these false teachers "dogs" (that's what some Jews called the Gentiles) and called circumcision "the concision" ("mutilation"), and he affirmed that Christian believers were the "true circumcision" (Phil. 3:1-3). God's children have experienced in Christ an inward "spiritual surgery" that has given them a new heart and new desires (2 Cor. 5:17; Eph. 4:24; Col. 3:10; see Ezek. 11:19; 36:26).

Just as the Jewish men at Gilgal had to submit to God's will, so believers today must yield to the Spirit and allow Him to make true in their personal experience what God says is true in His Word. We must practice "dead reckoning" (Rom. 6:11ff).

2. Remembering the Lord's goodness (Josh. 5:10-12)

"Forgetting those things which are behind" (Phil. 3:13) is wise counsel for most areas of life, but there are some things we must never forget. In his farewell address to the nation, Moses repeatedly commanded the Jews to remember that they were once slaves in Egypt and that the Lord had delivered them and made them His own people (Deut. 6:15; 15:15; 16:12; 24:18, 22). This great truth was embodied in their annual Passover feast. They were never to forget that they were a redeemed people, set free by the blood of the lamb.

Forty years before, Israel had celebrated the Passover on the night of their deliverance from Egypt (Ex. 11–14). They also celebrated Passover at Mt. Sinai, before leaving for Kadesh Barnea (Num. 9:1-14); but there is no evidence that they commemorated the Passover at any time during their years of wilderness wandering. The fact that the new generation wasn't circumcised prevented them from participating, and God had temporarily suspended His covenant with His people because of their rebellion at Kadesh Barnea. That one act of unbelief had cost Israel dearly.

The death of Jesus Christ is typified in the slaying of the Passover lamb (1 Cor. 5:7), and His resurrection is typified in the "wave offering" that was presented on the day after the Sabbath that followed Passover (Lev. 23:10-14; 1 Cor. 15:23). The day after the Sabbath would be the first day of the week, the Lord's Day, the day of Christ's resurrection (Matt. 28:1). Again, we see the picture of death and resurrection, which is our only means of life and victory (Rom. 6:4).

The Passover was followed by the Feast of Unleavened Bread when for a week the Jews avoided leaven (yeast) and ate unleavened bread (Ex. 12:15, 18-20). When Israel entered Canaan, it was time for the barley harvest; thus grain was available. No doubt the inhabitants of the area had left grain behind when they fled to Jericho for safety; thus that grain was also available. The Lord prepared a table for His people in the presence of their enemies, and Israel didn't have to be afraid (Ps. 23:5).

On the day after Passover, the manna ceased; and thus ended a forty-year miracle (Ex. 16). If the Passover reminded the Jews of their redemption from Egypt, the manna reminded them of their desire to go back to Egypt! "Would to God we had died by the hand of the Lord in the land of Egypt, when we sat by the flesh pots, and when we did eat bread to the full" (Ex. 16:3). God fed His people the bread of heaven, the food of the angels (Ps. 78:23-25); and yet they still lusted for the food of Egypt (Num. 11:4-9). God easily took His people out of Egypt, but it was difficult for Him to take Egypt out of His people.

Too many professed Christians contradict their profession by exhibiting an appetite for what belongs to their past life. "If then you were raised with Christ, seek those things which are above, where Christ is, sitting at the right hand of God. Set your mind on things above, not on things on the earth" (Col. 3:1-2, NKJV). Using the imagery from Joshua, this means, "You've crossed the river and are now in your inheritance. Don't look back and desire the things of Egypt or the wilderness. Let God feed you and satisfy you with the harvest in the inheritance."

The harvest is another image of death and resurrection. The seed is buried in the ground and *dies,* but from that death comes forth beauty and fruitfulness. Jesus applied to Himself both the image of the manna (John 6:26-59) and the harvest (12:20-28), for He is the nourishment upon which we must feed.

3. Reaffirming the Lord's presence (Josh. 5:13-15)
Joshua had read in the Book of the Law what Moses had said to the Lord after Israel had made the golden calf: "If Your

Presence does not go with us, do not bring us up from here" (Ex. 33:15, NKJV). The Lord had promised to be with Joshua just as He had been with Moses (Josh. 1:5), and now He reaffirmed that promise in a personal way. Like his predecessor, Joshua refused to move until he was sure the Lord's presence was with him.

This paragraph records one of the pre-incarnation appearances of the Lord Jesus Christ recorded in the Old Testament. To Abraham the pilgrim, the Lord came as a traveler to share in a friendly meal (Gen. 18:1-8). To Jacob the schemer, He came as a wrestler to bring him to the place of submission (32:24-32). The three Hebrew men met Him as their companion in the furnace of fire (Dan. 3:25), and Joshua met Him as the Captain of the Lord's armies. Our Lord always comes to us when we need Him and in the way we need Him.

It must have been a great encouragement to Joshua to realize that he was not alone. There is a loneliness to leadership that can be disturbing and even depressing as you realize how much your decisions affect the lives of others. "To be President of the United States is to be lonely," said Harry Truman, "very lonely at times of great decisions." Joshua must have been feeling some of that loneliness.

God had promised to be with Joshua (Josh. 1:5, 9), and the people had prayed that the Lord would be with him (vv. 16-17). The enemy knew that God was with Israel (2:8ff), and Joshua had encouraged his people with this promise (3:9ff). *Joshua was now experiencing the reality of that promise!* The Lord met him as Captain of the Lord's armies, whether in heaven or on earth. "The Lord of hosts [armies] is with us; the God of Jacob is our refuge" (Ps. 46:7, 11). Joshua would recall the song Israel had sung at the Red Sea: "The Lord is a man of war: the Lord is His name" (Ex. 15:3).

I appreciate the courage of Joshua as he confronted this stranger; for he wanted to know whose side he was on. With

Joshua, there was no compromise: You were either *for* the Lord and His people or *against* them (Matt. 12:30; Luke 11:23). When Joshua discovered the visitor was the Lord, he fell at His feet in worship and waited for His orders.

In Christian ministry great public victories are won in private as leaders submit to the Lord and receive their directions from Him. It's doubtful that anybody in the camp of Israel knew about their leader's meeting with the Lord, but that meeting made the difference between success and failure on the battlefield. The Chinese Bible teacher Watchman Nee wrote, "Not until we take the place of a servant can He take His place as Lord."

Joshua was reminded that *he was second in command.* Every father and mother, pastor, and Christian leader is second in command to the Lord Jesus Christ; and when we forget this fact, we start to move toward defeat and failure. The Lord came to Joshua that day, not just to help but *to lead.* "Without Me you can do nothing" (John 15:5, NKJV). Joshua was an experienced soldier, whom Moses had trained for leadership. Yet that was no guarantee of success. He needed the presence of the Lord God.

The Lord's first order to Joshua revealed to him that he was standing on holy ground. This reminds us of God's words to Moses at the burning bush (Ex. 3:5). Joshua was standing in "heathen territory"; yet because God was with him, *he was standing on holy ground.* If we are obeying the will of God, no matter where He leads us, we are on holy ground; *and we had better behave accordingly.* There's no such thing as "secular" and "sacred," "common" and "consecrated," when you are in the Lord's service. "Therefore, whether you eat or drink, or whatever you do, do all to the glory of God" (1 Cor. 10:31, NKJV).

The sequence here is significant: first *humble worship,* then *holy walk,* then *heavenly warfare.* This parallels the "spiritual postures" found in the Epistle to the Ephesians. Joshua first bowed the knee (Eph. 3:14); then he submitted to a holy walk (4:1, 17; 5:2, 8, 15); and then he went out to battle the enemy in the power of the Lord (6:10ff). Like Joshua, we have already been given our inheritance (described in Eph. 1–2) and we must overcome the enemy in order to claim it for ourselves and enjoy it.

When Joshua met the Lord, he discovered that *the battle was the Lord's and He had already overcome the enemy.* All Joshua had to do was listen to God's Word and obey orders, and God would do the rest. God had already given Jericho to Israel (Josh. 6:2); all they had to do was step out by faith and claim the victory by obeying the Lord.

In a meeting with a small group of missionaries in China, James Hudson Taylor, founder of the China Inland Mission (now Overseas Missionary Fellowship) reminded them that there were three ways to do God's work: "One is to make the best plans we can, and carry them out to the best of our ability . . . or, having carefully laid our plans and determined to carry them through, we may ask God to help us, and to prosper us in connection with them. Yet another way of working is to begin with God; to ask His plans, and to offer ourselves to Him to carry out His purposes."[1]

Joshua followed the third plan, and that's why the Lord blessed him.

The main lesson of Joshua 5 is that we must be a spiritually prepared people if we are going to do the Lord's work successfully and glorify His name. Instead of rushing into the battle, we must "take time to be holy."

In a letter to his missionary friend Rev. Daniel Edwards, the saintly Scottish preacher Robert Murray McCheyne wrote: "Remember you are God's sword — His instrument — I trust a chosen vessel unto Him to bear His name. In great measure, according to the purity and perfections of the instrument, will be the success. It is not great talents God blesses so much as great likeness to Jesus. A holy minister is an awful weapon in the hand of God."[2]

That letter was written in 1840, but its admonition applies to God's people today. All of us are His ministers, His servants; and we want to be holy instruments that He can use successfully.

Notes
1. Dr. and Mrs. Howard Taylor, *Biography of James Hudson Taylor* (London: China Inland Mission, 1965), p. 271.
2. Andrew A. Bonar, *Memoir and Remains of Robert Murray McCheyne* (London: Banner of Truth Trust, 1966), p. 282.

The Conquest Begins!

"**Y**ou are but a poor soldier of Christ if you think you can overcome without fighting, and suppose you can have the crown without the conflict."

The courageous Syrian preacher and martyr John Chrysostom (347–407) said that, and he was right; for the Christian life involves challenge and conflict whether we like it or not. Our enemies are constantly waging war against us and trying to keep us from claiming our inheritance in Jesus Christ. The world, the flesh, and the devil (Eph. 2:1-3) are united against Christ and His people just as the nations in Canaan were united against Joshua and the Jewish nation.

It's unfortunate that many of the "militant songs" of the church have been removed from some hymnals, apparently because the idea of warfare disturbs people and seems to contradict the words and works of Jesus Christ. But these zealous editors with scissors seem to have forgotten that the main theme of the Bible is God's holy warfare against Satan and sin. In Genesis 3:15, God declared war on Satan, and one day He will declare the victory when Jesus comes as Conqueror to establish His kingdom (Rev. 19:11-21). *If you eliminate the militant side of the Christian faith, then you must abandon the cross; for it was on the cross that Jesus won the victory over sin and Satan (Col. 2:13-15).*

A pastor attended a court hearing to protest the building of a tavern near his church and a public school. The lawyer for the tavern owners said to him, "I'm surprised to see you here today, Reverend. As a shepherd, shouldn't you be out taking care of the sheep?"

The pastor replied, "Today I'm fighting the wolf!"

Too many Christians cultivate only a sentimental emphasis on "peace and goodwill" and ignore the spiritual battle against sin; and this means they've already lost the victory and are working for the enemy. We must never forget Paul's warning about the savage wolves that are ready to destroy the flock (Acts 20:28-29).

The Christian's warfare is not against flesh and blood, but against enemies in the spiritual realm (Eph. 6:10-18); and the weapons we use are spiritual (2 Cor. 10:3-6). Satan and his demonic armies use people to oppose and attack the church of God; and if we don't take our stand with Christ, *we've already lost the battle.* In the army of Jesus Christ there can be no neutrality. "He that is not with Me is against Me," said Jesus; and He spoke those words in the context of spiritual warfare (Matt. 12:24-30). Since the Apostle Paul often used the military image to describe the Christian life, we dare not ignore the subject (Eph. 6:10ff; 2 Tim. 2:1-4; Rom. 13:12; 1 Thes. 5:8).

Israel's victory at Jericho illustrates three principles of spiritual conflict and victory applicable to our lives today, no matter what challenges we may be called to confront.

1. Before the challenge: remember that you fight *from* victory, not just *for* victory (Josh. 6:1-5)

The Christian soldier stands in a position of guaranteed victory because Jesus Christ has already defeated every spiritual enemy (John 12:31). Jesus defeated Satan not only in the wilderness (Matt. 4:1-11), but also during His earthly ministry (12:22-29), on the cross (Col. 2:13-15), and in His resurrection and ascension (Eph. 1:19-23). As He intercedes for His people in heaven, He helps us mature and accomplish His will (Heb. 13:20-21); and "if God be for us, who can be against us?" (Rom. 8:31)

Consider the factors involved in Joshua's victory:

The fear of the Lord (Josh. 6:1). The land of Canaan was divided up among a number of "city states," each ruled by a king (see 12:9-34). These cities were not large; Ai, which was smaller than Jericho (7:2-3), had about 12,000 people (8:25). Excavations at Jericho indicate that the city covered perhaps eight acres and was protected by two high parallel walls, which stood about fifteen feet apart and surrounded the city. It was the sight of cities like Jericho that convinced ten of the Jewish spies that Israel could never conquer the land (Num. 13:28).

But the news of Israel's exodus from Egypt and their recent victories east of the Jordan had already spread to Canaan and put the people in panic (Josh. 2:9-11; see Deut. 2:25; 7:23; 11:25; 32:30). "I will send My fear before you," God had promised; "I will cause confusion among all the people to whom you come, and will make all your enemies turn their backs to you" (Ex. 23:27, NKJV).

It was said that Mary Queen of Scots feared John Knox's prayers more than she feared an enemy army. But is society today afraid of what God's people may do? Probably not, and it's mainly because the church hasn't done very much to display the power of God to a skeptical world. The church is no longer "terrible as an army with banners" (Song 6:4, 10). In fact, the church is so much like the world that the world takes little notice of what we do. We imitate the world's methods; we cater to the world's appetites; we solicit the world's approval; and we measure what we do according to the world's standards. Is it any wonder that we don't gain the world's respect?

But not so with Joshua and Israel! They were a conquering people who made no compromise with the enemy but trusted God to give them the victory. Theirs was a march of triumph that put the fear of God into the hearts of the enemy.

The promise of the Lord (Josh 6:2). It's possible that the Lord spoke these words to Joshua when He confronted him at Jericho (5:13-15). The tense of the verb is important: *"I have given* Jericho into your hand" (6:2, NKJV, italics added). The victory had already been won! All Joshua and his people had to do was claim the promise and obey the Lord.

Victorious Christians are people who *know* the promises of God, because they spend time meditating on God's Word (1:8); they *believe* the promises of God, because the Word of God generates faith in their hearts (Rom. 10:17); and they *reckon* on these promises and obey what God tells them to do. To "reckon" means to count as true in your life what God says about you in His Word.

"Be of good cheer," Jesus told His disciples; "I have overcome the world" (John 16:33). "And they that are Christ's have crucified the flesh with the affections and lusts" (Gal. 5:24). "Now is the judgment of this world; now shall the prince of this world be cast out" (John 12:31). Christ has conquered the world, the flesh, and the devil; *and if we reckon on this truth, we can conquer through Him.* It's possible to *believe* a promise and still not *reckon on it* and obey the Lord. Believing a promise is like accepting a check, but reckoning is like endorsing the check and cashing it.

The instructions of the Lord (Josh. 6:3-5). "Joshua did not take the city merely by a clever, human military tactic," wrote Francis A. Schaeffer. "The strategy was the Lord's."[1]

No situation is too great for the Lord to handle, and no

problem is too much for Him to solve. When He saw more than 5,000 hungry people before Him, Jesus asked Philip, "Where shall we buy bread, that these may eat?" Then John adds, "But this He said to test him; for He Himself knew what He would do" (John 6:5-6, NKJV). *God always knows what He will do.* Our responsibility is to wait for Him to tell us all that we need to know and then obey it.

At the close of the last chapter, I quoted J. Hudson Taylor's words about three different ways to serve the Lord: (1) to make the best plans we can and hope they succeed; (2) to make our own plans and ask God to bless them; or (3) to ask God for His plans and then do what He tells us to do. Joshua received his orders from the Lord, and that's why Israel succeeded.

God's plan for the conquest of Jericho was seemingly foolish, but it worked. God's wisdom is far above ours (Isa. 55:8-9) and He delights in using people and plans that seem foolish to the world (1 Cor. 1:26-29). Whether it's Joshua with trumpets, Gideon with torches and pitchers (Jud. 7), or David with his sling (1 Sam. 17), God delights in using weakness and seeming foolishness to defeat His enemies and glorify His name. "For the eyes of the Lord run to and fro throughout the whole earth, to shew Himself strong in the behalf of them whose heart is perfect toward Him" (2 Chron. 16:9).

God's instructions were that the armed men march around Jericho once a day for six days, followed by seven priests each blowing a trumpet. The priests carrying the ark of the Lord would come next, and the rear guard would complete the procession. The only noise permitted was the sound of the trumpets. On the seventh day the procession would march around the city seven times, the priests would give a long blast on the trumpets, and then the marchers would all shout. God would then cause the walls to fall down flat so that the soldiers could easily enter the city.

In this plan the emphasis is on the number seven: seven priests, seven trumpets, seven days of marching, and seven circuits of the city on the seventh day. The number seven is written clearly into the life of Israel: The Sabbath celebrated on the seventh day of the week; seven weeks from Passover is Pentecost; the seventh year is the Sabbatical Year; and after forty-nine years (seven times seven) comes the Year of Jubilee. Three of Israel's feasts fall in the seventh month: the Feast of Trumpets, the Day of Atonement (Lev. 16), and the Feast of Tabernacles. (For details about this remarkable calendar, see Lev. 23.)

In biblical numerology the number seven represents completeness or perfection. The Hebrew word translated "seven" *(shevah)* comes from a root that means "to be full, to be satisfied." When God finished His work of creation, He rested on the seventh day and sanctified it (Gen. 2:3); and this helped give the number seven its sacred significance. The Jews noted that there were seven promises in God's covenant with Abraham (12:1-3) and seven branches on the candlestick in the tabernacle (Ex. 37:17-24). Anything involving the number seven was especially sacred to them. It spoke of God's ability to finish whatever He started.

The Jews used two different kinds of trumpets, those made of silver and those made of ram's horns. The silver trumpets were used especially by the priests to signal the camp when something important was happening (Num. 10). The ram's horns were used primarily for celebrations. The common Hebrew word for "trumpet" is *shofar;* for "ram's horn," it is *jobel,* which is the root of the word *jubilee.* The "Year of Jubilee" was the fiftieth year after seven Sabbaticals, and was a special time of celebration in Israel (Lev. 25; 27:17-14). The priests blew the ram's horns to "proclaim liberty throughout all the land" (25:10).

The priests didn't use the silver trumpets in this event

because Israel was not declaring war on Jericho, *for there was no war!* The Jews were announcing the arrival of the "Year of Jubilee" for Israel in their new land. God's people today can march in triumphal procession because of the victory of Jesus Christ over all the enemies of God (Rom. 8:37; 2 Cor. 2:14; Col. 2:15). We should be living like victors, not victims.

"The wall of the city shall fall down!" (Josh. 6:5) was God's promise, and His promises never fail (21:45; 23:14). God's people don't simply fight *for* victory but *from* victory, because the Lord has already won the battle. Reckon on His promises and obey what He tells you to do, and you shall have the victory.

2. During the challenge: Remember that you overcome the enemy by faith (Josh. 6:6-16, 20)
"By faith the walls of Jericho fell down, after they were compassed about seven days" (Heb. 11:30). "And this is the victory that has overcome the world—our faith" (1 John 5:4, NKJV).

Faith is not believing in spite of evidence, for the people of Israel had been given one demonstration after another proving that God's Word and God's power can be trusted. The Lord had opened the Red Sea, destroyed the Egyptian army, cared for His people in the wilderness, defeated great kings, given Israel their land, opened the Jordan River, and brought His people safely into the Promised Land. How could they do anything other than believe Him!

Joshua first shared the Lord's plan with the priests. It was important that the ark of the Lord be in its proper place, for it represented the presence of the Lord with His people. When Israel crossed the river, the account mentions the ark sixteen times (Josh. 3–4); and here in 6:6-15, the ark is mentioned eight times. Israel could march and the priests blow trumpets until all of them dropped from weariness; but if the Lord wasn't with them, there would be no victory. *When we accept God's plan, we invite God's presence; and that guarantees victory.* (See Ex. 33:12-17.)

Then Joshua instructed the soldiers. He probably didn't enlist the entire army for this important event; for that would have involved far too many people. According to the military census of Numbers 26, there were over 600,000 men able to bear arms. Think of how long it would take that many men to march around the city walls! And when the walls fell down, Joshua certainly didn't need hundreds of thousands of soldiers to rush in and overcome the people. The men would have been falling over one another!

Over 2 million people were in the nation of Israel, and marching all of them around the city of Jericho would have been time-consuming and dangerous. The people no doubt watched in silence from a distance and then participated in the great shout on the seventh day. It was a victory for Israel and Israel's God, and not just for the priests and soldiers.

It's important that leaders receive their orders from the Lord and that those who follow them obey their instructions. As with the crossing of the Jordan River, so also the conquest of Jericho was a miracle of faith. Joshua and his people listened to God's orders, believed them, and obeyed; and God did the rest. When God's people rebel against spiritual leadership, as Israel often did in the wilderness, it leads to discipline and defeat.

The activities of the week were a test of the Jewish people's faith and patience. No doubt some of them were anxious to get on with the invasion so they could claim their inheritance and settle down to enjoy the rest God had promised them (Josh. 1:13). To some of them, it may have seemed a futile waste of time to devote an entire week to the taking of one city. Impatience was one of Israel's besetting sins, and God was helping them learn patient obedience; for it's through "faith and patience" that God's people inherit what He has promised (Heb. 6:12). *God is never in a hurry.* He knows what He's doing, and His timing is never off.

If the week's schedule was a test of their patience, the divine command of silence was a test of their self-control. People who can't control their tongues can't control their bodies (James 3:1-2), and what good are soldiers whose bodies are not disciplined? "Be still, and know that I am God" (Ps. 46:10). In the Christian life there's "a time to keep silence, and a time to speak" (Ecc. 3:7); and wise is the child of God who knows the difference. Our Lord is the perfect example of this (Isa. 53:7; Matt. 26:62-63; 27:14; Luke 23:9).

How did the people in the city of Jericho respond to this daily procession around the city? It's likely that the march on the first day frightened them, for they probably expected the army to raise a siege against the city. But the Jews neither built ramps against the walls nor did they try to batter down the gates. When the marchers returned to camp after making only one circuit of the walls, the citizens must have felt greatly relieved. However, as the march was repeated day after day, tension must have grown in the city as the people wondered what would happen next. They knew that the God of Israel was a "great God of wonders," whose power had defeated Egypt and the kings east of the Jordan. What would Jehovah now do to Jericho?

When the procession went around the walls seven times on the seventh day, the tension within the city must have increased to frightening proportions. Then came the blast of the trumpets and the victory shout of the people, *and the walls fell down flat!* All that the soldiers had to do was rush into the city and take over.

The Holy Spirit directed the writer of the Epistle to the Hebrews to use this event as one of the "by faith" examples in Hebrews 11. The fall of Jericho is an encouragement to

God's people to trust the Lord's promises and obey His instructions, no matter how impossible the situation may appear to be. You and I may not capture a city as Joshua did, but in our everyday lives we face enemies and high walls that challenge us. *The only way to grow in faith is to accept new challenges and trust God to give you victory.* "Do not pray for easy lives," said Phillips Brooks; "pray to be better men and women. Do not pray for tasks equal to your powers; pray for power equal to your tasks."

3. **After the victory: Remember to obey God's commands and give Him the glory (Josh. 6:17-19, 21-17)**
Let me quote again Andrew Bonar's wise counsel: "Let us be as watchful after the victory as before the battle." Because one soldier didn't heed this warning, Israel's next challenge in Canaan turned out to be a humiliating defeat. Joshua gave the soldiers four instructions to obey after they had taken the city.

Devote the entire city to God (Josh. 6:17-19). This meant that everything was dedicated to the Lord—the people, the houses, the animals, and all the spoils of war—and He could do with it whatever He pleased. In this first victory in Canaan, Jericho was presented to God as "the firstfruits" of the victories to come. Ordinarily the soldiers shared the spoils of war (Deut. 20:14), but not at Jericho; for everything there belonged to the Lord and was put into His treasury (Deut. 13:16; 1 Kings 7:51). It was this command that Achan disobeyed, and his disobedience later brought Israel defeat and disgrace and brought Achan and his family death.

Rescue Rahab and her family (Josh. 6:22-23, 25-26). When the walls of the city fell down, it appears that the section of the wall that held Rahab's house (2:15) *didn't fall down!* It wasn't necessary for the spies to look for a window with a red cord hanging from it (vv. 18-19), because the only house that was preserved was the house in which Rahab and her family waited. When the spies made their covenant with Rahab, they didn't know exactly how God would give them the city.

God saved and protected Rahab because of her faith (Heb. 11:31); and because she led her family to trust in Jehovah, they were also saved. These Gentile believers were rescued from a fiery judgment because they trusted the God of Israel, for "salvation is of the Jews" (John 4:22). They were "afar off" as far as the covenants were concerned (Eph. 2:11-12), but their faith brought them into the nation of Israel; for Rahab married Salmon and became an ancestress of King David *and of the Messiah!* (Matt. 1:5)

Rahab and her relatives were put "outside the camp" initially because they were unclean Gentiles, and "outside the camp" was the place designated for the unclean (Num. 5:1-4; 12:14; Deut. 23:9-14). The men in the family would have to be circumcised in order to become "sons of the covenant," and all of the family would have to submit to the Law of Moses. What grace that God spared Rahab and her loved ones, and what *abundant* grace that He chose her, an outcast Gentile, to be an ancestress of the Savior!

Like Jericho of old, our present world is under the judgment of God (John 3:18-21; Rom. 3:10-19); and His judgment will eventually fall. No matter what "walls" and "gates" this present evil world will try to hide behind, God's wrath will eventually meet them. God has given this lost world plenty of evidence so that sinners can believe and be saved (Josh. 2:8-13; Rom. 1:18ff). The tragedy is, lost sinners willingly reject the evidence and continue in their sins (John 12:35-41).

Destroy the people (Josh. 6:21). It disturbs some people that God commanded every living thing in Jericho to be killed. Isn't our God a God of mercy? After all, it's one thing for the Jews to kill the enemy soldiers; but why kill women, children, and even animals?

To begin with, this commandment was not a new one. The Lord had given it to Moses years before. In the "divine law of war" found in Deuteronomy 20, the Lord made a distinction between attacking cities that were far off (vv. 10-15) and cities in the land of Canaan where Israel would dwell (vv. 16-18). Before besieging a city afar off, the Jews were to give that city an offer of peace; and if the city surrendered, the Jews would spare the people and make them subjects. But the people in the cities *in the land of Canaan* were to be destroyed completely, and their cities burned.

Why? For one thing, the civilization in Canaan was unspeakably wicked; and God didn't want His holy people contaminated by their neighbors (7:1-11). We must never forget that God put Israel in the world to be the channel for His blessing (Gen. 12:1-3), which involves, among other things, the writing of the Scriptures and the coming of the Savior. Read the Old Testament record, and you will see Satan doing everything he could to pollute the Jewish nation and thus prevent the birth of the Messiah. When the Jewish men married pagan women and began to worship pagan gods, it was a threat to the purposes God had for His chosen people (Neh. 13:23-31). God wanted a "holy seed" (Mal. 2:14-15) so that His holy Son could come to be the Savior of the world.

"God is perpetually at war with sin," said G. Campbell Morgan. "That is the whole explanation of the extermination of the Canaanites."[2] Because the Jews didn't fully obey this commandment in later years, it led to national defilement and divine chastening (Ps. 106:34-48). The Book of Judges would not be in the Bible if the nation of Israel had remained true to the Lord (Jud. 2:11-23).

There is a second consideration: The people in the land had been given plenty of opportunity to repent and turn to the Lord, just as Rahab and her family had done. God patiently endured the evil of the Canaanites from the time of Abraham (Gen. 15:16) to the time of Moses, a period of over 400 years. (See 2 Peter 3:9.) From the Exodus to the crossing of the Jordan was another 40 years in Israel's history, *and the Canaanites knew what was going on!* (See Josh. 2:8-13.) Every wonder that God performed and every victory that God gave His people was a witness to the people of the land, but they preferred to go on in their sins and reject the mercy of God. Never think of the Canaanites as helpless ignorant people who knew nothing about the true God. They were willfully sinning against a flood of light.

We should also keep in mind that these historical events were written "for our learning" (Rom. 15:4) as we seek to live for Christ today. In the destruction of Jericho and its population God is telling us that *He will tolerate no compromise with sin in the lives of His people.* To quote Campbell Morgan again: "Thank God that He will not make peace with sin in my heart! I bless His name for the thunder of His authority, and for the profound conviction that He is fierce and furious in His anger against sin, wherever it manifests itself."[3]

When I was a child in Sunday School, the superintendent often chose the song "Whiter Than Snow" for us to sing in general assembly. While we sang "Break down every idol/Cast out every foe," I confess that I didn't understand at the time what I was singing; but now I understand. *The Lord will not share my life if there are rival gods in my heart. He will not permit me to compromise with the enemy.* When you grasp this truth, you also better understand His admonition in 2 Corinthians 6:14–7:1.

Burn the city (Josh. 6:24). "Thy God is a consuming fire" was spoken by Moses in Deuteronomy 4:24 long before it was quoted by the Holy Spirit in Hebrews 12:29. Moses was warning the Jewish people against idolatry and the danger of following the religious practices of the people in Canaan. Moses added a phrase that isn't quoted in Hebrews but is still important for us to know: "even a jealous God." God is jealous over His people and will not permit them to divide their love and service between Him and the false gods of the world (Ex. 20:5; 34:14). We cannot serve two masters.

Jericho was a wicked city, *and sin is only fuel for the holy wrath of God.* Jesus compared hell to a furnace of fire (Matt. 13:42), fire that is eternal (25:41, 46); and John compared it to a lake of fire (Rev. 19:20; 20:10, 14). John the Baptist described God's judgment as "unquenchable fire" (Matt. 3:12). The burning of Jericho, like the destruction of Sodom and Gomorrah (Jude 7), is a picture of the judgment of God that will fall on all who reject the truth.

Even after he had burned the city, Joshua put a curse on Jericho. This would warn any of the Jews or Rahab's descendants who might be tempted to rebuild what God had destroyed. The curse was later fulfilled in the days of evil King Ahab (1 Kings 16:34).

As He promised, God was with Joshua (Josh. 1:5, 9); and God magnified Joshua's name in the land (v. 27; 3:7; 4:14). God's servants must never magnify themselves; and if the Lord magnifies them, they must be careful to give Him the glory. It's when we are strong that we get overconfident and forget to trust the Lord (2 Chron. 26:15).

Notes

1. Francis A. Schaeffer, *Joshua and the Flow of Biblical History* (Downers Grove, Ill.: InterVarsity Press, 1975), pp. 102–3.
2. G. Campbell Morgan, *Living Messages of the Books of the Bible* (Old Tappan, N.J.: Fleming H. Revell, 1912), vol. 1, p. 104.
3. Ibid., p. 114.

Defeat in the Land of Victory

Moses described the Promised Land as "a land of hills and valleys" (Deut. 11:11). That statement, I believe, is much more than a description of the contrast between the hilly landscape of Canaan and the flat monotonous topography of Egypt. It's also a description of the *geography* of the life of faith that is pictured by Israel's experiences in Canaan. As by faith we claim our inheritance in Christ, we experience peaks of victory and valleys of discouragement. Discouragement isn't inevitable in the Christian life, but we must remember that we can't have mountains without valleys.

The ominous word *but* that introduces Joshua 7 is a signal that things are going to change; for Joshua is about to descend from the mountaintop of victory at Jericho to the valley of defeat at Ai. Joshua was a gifted and experienced leader, but he was still human and therefore liable to error. In this experience, he teaches us what causes defeat and how we must handle the discouragements of life.

1. A disobedient soldier (Josh. 7:1, 20-21)
The sinner (Josh. 7:1). His name was Achan, or Achar, which means "trouble"; and he was from the tribe of Judah (v. 16).

(See 1 Chron. 2:7; note in v. 26 that "Achor" also means "trouble.") He is known in Bible history as *the man who troubled Israel* (Josh. 7:25). Because of Achan's disobedience, Israel was defeated at Ai, and the enemy killed thirty-six Jewish soldiers. It was Israel's first and only military defeat in Canaan, a defeat that is forever associated with Achan's name.

Never underestimate the amount of damage one person can do outside the will of God. Abraham's disobedience in Egypt almost cost him his wife (Gen. 12:10-20); David's disobedience in taking an unauthorized census led to the death of 70,000 people (2 Sam. 24); and Jonah's refusal to obey God almost sank a ship (Jonah 1). The church today must look diligently "lest any root of bitterness springing up cause trouble" (Heb. 12:15, NKJV). That's why Paul admonished the Corinthian believers to discipline the disobedient man in their fellowship, because his sin was defiling the whole church (1 Cor. 5).

God made it clear that it was *Israel* that had sinned and not just Achan alone (Josh. 7:1, 11). Why would God blame the whole nation for the disobedience of only one soldier? Because Israel was *one people in the Lord* and not just an assorted collection of tribes, clans, families, and individuals. God dwelt in the midst of their camp, and this made the Jews the Lord's special people (Ex. 19:5-6). Jehovah God walked about in their camp, and therefore the camp was to be kept holy (Deut. 23:14). Anyone who disobeyed God defiled the camp, and this defilement affected their relationship to the Lord and to one another.

God's people today are one body in Christ. Consequently, we belong to each other, we need each other, and we affect each other (1 Cor. 12:12ff). Any weakness or infection in one part of the human body contributes to weakness and infection in the other parts. So it also is with the body of Christ. "If one part suffers, every part suffers with it; if one part is honored, every part rejoices with it" (1 Cor. 12:26, NIV). "One sinner destroys much good" (Ecc. 9:18, NKJV).

The sin (Josh. 7:20-21). Achan heard his commander give the order that all the spoils in Jericho were to be devoted to the Lord and were to go into His treasury (6:17-21, 24). Since Jericho was Israel's first victory in Canaan, the firstfruits of the spoils belonged to the Lord (Prov. 3:9). But Achan disobeyed and took the hazardous steps that lead to sin and death (James 1:13-15): "I saw...I coveted...[I] took" (Josh. 7:21). Eve did the same thing when she listened to *the devil* (Gen. 3:5), and so did David when he yielded to *the flesh* (2 Sam. 11:1-4). Since Achan also coveted the things of *the world,* he brought defeat to Israel and death to himself and his family.

Achan's first mistake was to look at these spoils a *second time.* He probably couldn't help seeing them the first time, but he should never have looked again and considered taking them. A man's first glance at a woman may say to him, "She's attractive!" But it's that second glance that gets the imagination working and leads to sin (Matt. 6:27-30). If we keep God's Word before our eyes, we won't start looking in the wrong direction and doing the wrong things (Prov. 4:20-25).

His second mistake was to *reclassify* those treasures and call them "the spoils" (Josh. 7:21). They were not "the spoils"; they were a part of the Lord's treasury and wholly dedicated to Him. They didn't belong to Achan, or even to Israel; they belonged to God. When God identifies something in a special way, we have no right to change it. In our world today, including the religious world, people are rewriting God's dictionary! "Woe unto them that call evil good, and good evil; that put darkness for light, and light for darkness; that put bitter for sweet, and sweet for bitter!" (Isa. 5:20, KJV)

If God says something is wrong, then it's wrong; and that's the end of the debate.

Achan's third mistake was to *covet*. "But each one is tempted when he is drawn away by his own desires and enticed" (James 1:14, NKJV). Instead of singing praises in his heart for the great victory God had given, Achan was imagining in his heart what it would be like to own all that treasure. The imagination is the "womb" in which desire is conceived and from which sin and death are eventually born.

His fourth mistake was to think that he could get away with his sin by hiding the loot. Adam and Eve tried to cover their sin and run away and hide, but the Lord discovered them (Gen. 3:7ff). "Be sure your sin will find you out" was originally said to the people of God, not to the lost (Num. 32:23); and so was "The Lord shall judge His people" (Deut. 32:36; Heb. 10:30). How foolish of Achan to think that God couldn't see what he was doing, when "all things are naked and open to the eyes of Him to whom we must give account" (Heb. 4:13, NKJV).

Achan's sin becomes even more odious when you stop to realize all that God had done for him. God had cared for him and his family in the wilderness. He had brought them safely across the Jordan and given the army victory at Jericho. The Lord had accepted Achan as a son of the covenant at Gilgal. Yet in spite of all these wonderful experiences, Achan disobeyed God just to possess some wealth that he couldn't even enjoy. Had he waited just a day or two, he could have gathered all the spoils he wanted from the victory at Ai! "But seek first the kingdom of God and His righteousness, and all these things shall be added to you" (Matt. 6:33, NKJV).

2. A defeated army (Josh. 7:2-5)
Like every good commander, Joshua surveyed the situation before he planned his strategy (Num. 21:32; Prov. 20:18;

24:6). His mistake wasn't in sending out the spies but in assuming that the Lord was pleased with His people and would give them victory over Ai. He and his officers were walking by sight and not by faith. Spiritual leaders must constantly seek the Lord's face and determine what His will is for each new challenge. Had Joshua called a prayer meeting, the Lord would have informed him that there was sin in the camp; and Joshua could have dealt with it. This would have saved the lives of thirty-six soldiers and spared Israel a humiliating defeat.

It's impossible for us to enter into Joshua's mind and fully understand his thinking. No doubt the impressive victory at Jericho had given Joshua and his army a great deal of self-confidence; and self-confidence can lead to presumption. Since Ai was a smaller city than Jericho, victory seemed inevitable from the human point of view. But instead of seeking the mind of the Lord, Joshua accepted the counsel of his spies; and this led to defeat. He would later repeat this mistake in his dealings with the Gibeonites (Josh. 9).

The spies said nothing about the Lord; their whole report focused on the army and their confidence that Israel would have victory. You don't hear these men saying, "If the Lord will" (James 4:13-17). They were sure that the whole army wasn't needed for the assault, but that wasn't God's strategy when He gave the orders for the second attack on Ai (Josh. 8:1). Since God's thoughts are not our thoughts (Isa. 55:8-9), we'd better take time to seek His direction. "Pride goes before destruction, and a haughty spirit before a fall" (Prov. 16:18, NKJV). What Israel needed was God-confidence, not self-confidence.

Ai was in the hill country, about fifteen miles from Jericho; and one went *up* to Ai because it was situated 1,700 feet above sea level. The Jewish army marched confidently up the hill but soon came down again, fleeing for their lives and leaving thirty-six dead comrades behind them.

Moses had warned Israel that they couldn't defeat their enemies unless the nation was obedient to the Lord. If they were following the Lord by faith, 1 Jewish soldier would chase 1,000, and 2 would put 10,000 to flight! (Deut. 32:30) Three Jewish soldiers could have defeated the whole city, if the nation had been pleasing to the Lord (Josh. 8:25). "But your iniquities have separated between you and your God, and your sins have hid His face from you, that He will not hear" (Isa. 59:2).

3. A discouraged leader (Josh. 7:6-15)

The leader who had been magnified (6:27) was now mortified. If some of your best plans have ever been dashed to pieces, then you can identify with Joshua and his officers.

Remorse (Josh. 7:6). The hearts of the Canaanites had melted when they had heard about the conquests of Israel (2:11). But now the tables were turned, and it was the Jews whose hearts were melted as water! The general who had not known defeat spent the rest of the day prostrate before the ark at Gilgal and his leaders with him. They tore their garments, put dust on their heads, lay on the ground, and cried, "Alas! Alas!" This is the way Jewish people behaved whenever they experienced great distress, such as a military defeat (1 Sam. 4:12) or personal violence and shame (2 Sam. 13:19). It was the prescribed course of action whenever the Jews turned to God in times of great danger or national sin (Neh. 9:1; Es. 4:1). Had Joshua humbled himself *before* the battle, the situation would have been different after the battle.

The ark of the covenant was a reminder of the presence of God with His people. The ark had gone before Israel when they had crossed the river (Josh. 3:11ff), and the ark had been with them when they had marched around Jericho (6:6-8). God hadn't told them to carry the ark to Ai, but God's presence would have gone with them if there had not been sin in the camp. Without God's presence, the ark was simply a piece of wooden furniture; and there was no guarantee of victory just because of the presence of the ark (1 Sam. 4).

Reproach (Josh. 7:7-9). In his prayer Joshua sounded like the unbelieving Jews whenever they found themselves in a tough situation that demanded faith: "Oh, that we had stayed where we were!" They said this at the Red Sea (Ex. 14:11), when they were hungry and thirsty in the wilderness (16:3; 17:3), and when they were disciplined at Kadesh Barnea (Num. 14:1-3). The Jews had frequently wanted to go back to Egypt, but Joshua would have been willing to cross the Jordan and settle down on the other side.

"But read his prayer, and you will catch a strange note in it," wrote George H. Morrison; *"Joshua reproaches God."*[1] He seems to be blaming God for Israel's presence in Canaan and for the humiliating defeat they had just experienced.

When you walk by faith, you will claim all that God has for you; *but unbelief is always content to settle for something less than God's best.* This is why the Epistle to the Hebrews is in the Bible, to urge God's people to "go on" and enter into the fullness of their inheritance in Christ (Heb. 6:1). God sometimes permits us to experience humiliating defeats in order to test our faith and reveal to us what's really going on in our hearts. What life does *to* us depends on what life finds *in* us, and we don't always know the condition of our own hearts (Jer. 17:9).

Repentance (Josh. 7:8-9). Now Joshua gets to the heart of the matter: Israel's defeat had robbed God of glory, and for this they had to repent. If the people of the land lost their fear of Israel's God (2:8-11), this would make it difficult for Joshua to conquer the land. But the important thing was not Joshua's fame or Israel's conquests, but the glory of the God of Israel. Joshua's concern was not for his own reputation but for the "great name" of Jehovah. Joshua had learned this lesson from Moses (Ex. 32:11-13; Num. 14:13-16), and it's a lesson the church needs to learn today.

Rebuke (Josh. 7:10-15). The Lord allowed Joshua and his leaders to stay on their faces until the time for the evening sacrifice. He gave them time to come to the end of themselves so that they would obey His directions, and then He spoke to Joshua. There is a time to pray and a time to act, and the time had now come to act.

Since Israel had sinned, Israel had to deal with its sin. God told Joshua that the nation had stolen that which belonged to Him and had hidden it among their own possessions as if it were theirs. Note the repetition of the word "accursed," which is used six times in this paragraph. The nation had been sanctified in preparation for crossing the Jordan (3:5), but now they had to be sanctified to discover an enemy in the camp. They had to present themselves to God so He could expose the guilty man.

What the Lord said to Joshua helps us see Achan's sin (and Israel's sin) from the divine point of view. What they did was *sin* (7:11), a word that means "to miss the mark." God wants His people to be holy and obedient, but they missed the mark and fell short of God's standard. It was also *transgression* (v. 11), which means "to cross over." God had drawn a line and told them not to cross it, but they had violated His covenant and crossed the line.

This sin involved *stealing from God* and then *lying about it* (v. 11). Achan had taken the forbidden wealth but pretended that he had obeyed the Lord. Achan had done a foolish thing (v. 15) in thinking he could rob God and get away with it. Israel couldn't face any of her enemies until their sin had been put away. The tribes could never claim their inheritance as long as one man clung to his forbidden treasures. Everything God had done for His people up to this point was to no avail as long as they couldn't go forward in victory. What a lesson for the church today!

That evening Joshua sent word throughout the camp that the people were to sanctify themselves and prepare for an assembly to be held the next morning. You wonder whether Achan and his family got any sleep that night, or did they think they were secure?

4. A discovered sinner (Josh. 7:16-26)

The investigation (Josh. 7:16-18). "The heart is deceitful above all things, and desperately wicked: who can know it?" asked the prophet (Jer. 17:9); and he answered the question in the next verse: "I the Lord search the heart, I try the reins, even to give every man according to his ways, and according to the fruit of his doings."

Nobody can hide from God. "Can any hide himself in secret places that I shall not see him?" (23:24) Whether sinners run to the top of the mountains or dive to the bottom of the seas, God will find them and judge them (Amos 9:3). "For God shall bring every work into judgment, with every secret thing, whether it be good, or whether it be evil" (Ecc. 12:14).

God's approach was methodical. First He singled out the tribe of Judah, then the family of the Zerahites, then the household of Zabdi, and finally the culprit Achan. Perhaps the high priest used the ephod to determine God's direction (1 Sam. 23:6, 9; 30:7-8), or Joshua and the high priest may have cast lots. It must have been frightening for Achan and his immediate family to watch the accusing finger of God point closer and closer. "My eyes are on all their ways; they are not hidden from Me, nor is their sin concealed from My eyes" (Jer. 16:17, NIV). Read Psalm 10, especially verses 6, 11, 13 to see what may have been going on in Achan's mind and heart during this tense time of scrutiny.

When Joshua singled out Achan as the offender, the people

watching must have asked themselves, "What evil thing did he do that the Lord was so displeased with us?" Perhaps the relatives of the thirty-six slain soldiers were angry as they looked at the man whose disobedience caused the death of their loved ones.

The confession (Josh. 7:19-23). The phrase "Give glory to God" was a form of official oath in Israel (John 9:24, NIV). Achan had not only sinned against his own people, but also he had grievously sinned against the Lord; and he had to confess his sin to Him. When he said "I have sinned," he joined the ranks of seven other men in Scripture who made the same confession, some more than once, and some without sincerity: Pharaoh (Ex. 9:27; 10:16), Balaam (Num. 22:34), King Saul (1 Sam. 15:24, 30; 26:21), David (2 Sam. 12:13; 24:10, 17; Ps. 51:4), Shimei (2 Sam. 19:20), Judas (Matt. 27:4), and the prodigal son (Luke 15:18, 21).

Before he could execute the Lord's judgment, Joshua had to present the evidence that substantiated Achan's confession. The messengers dug under Achan's tent and found "the accursed thing" that had brought defeat to Israel. The stolen goods were spread out before the Lord so He could see that all Israel was renouncing their hold on this evil treasure. The confession and the evidence were enough to convict the accused man.

The judgment (Josh. 7:24-26). Since a law in Israel prohibited innocent family members from being punished for the sins of their relatives (Deut. 24:16), Achan's family must have been guilty of assisting him in his sin. His household was judged the same way Israel would deal with a Jewish city that had turned to idols (Josh. 13:12-18). Achan and his family had turned from the true and living God and had given their hearts to that which God had said was accursed—silver, gold, and an expensive garment. It wasn't worth it!

At the beginning of a new period in Bible history, God

sometimes revealed His wrath against sin in some dramatic way. After the tabernacle had been set up, Nadab and Abihu invaded its holy precincts contrary to God's law; and God killed them. This was a warning to the priests not to treat God's sanctuary carelessly (Lev. 10). When David sought to restore the ark to its place of honor, and Uzzah touched the ark to steady it, God killed Uzzah (2 Sam. 6:1-11); another warning from God not to treat sacred things carelessly. At the beginning of the Church Age, when Ananias and Sapphira lied to God and God's people, the Lord killed them (Acts 5:1-11).

The death of Achan and his family was certainly a dramatic warning to the nation not to take the Word of God lightly. The people and the animals were stoned, and their bodies burned along with all that the family possessed. The troubler of Israel was completely removed from the scene, the people were sanctified, and now God could march with His people and give them victory. The name *Achor* means "trouble." The Valley of Achor is mentioned in Isaiah 65:10 and Hosea 2:15 as a place where the Jews will one day have a new beginning and no longer be associated with shame and defeat. The Valley of Achor will become for them "a door of hope" when they return to their land and share in the blessings of the messianic kingdom. How wonderful the Lord is to take Achor, a place of sorrow and defeat, and make it into a place of hope and joy.

The heap of stones in the valley would be a reminder that God expects His people to obey His Word, and if they don't, He must judge them. The heap of stones at Gilgal (Josh. 4:1-8) reminded them that God keeps His Word and leads His obedient people to the place of blessing. Both memorials are needed in the walk of faith. God is love (1 John 4:8, 16) and longs to bless His people; but God is also light (1 John 1:5) and must judge His people's sins.

It had been a trying two days for Joshua and his leaders, but the situation was about to change. God would take charge of the army and lead His people to victory. When you surrender to the Lord, no defeat is permanent and no mistake is beyond remedy. Even the "Valley of Trouble" can become a "door of hope."

Notes
1. George H. Morrison, *The Footsteps of the Flock* (London: Hodder and Stoughton, 1904), p. 106.

Turning Defeat into Victory

The following quotation runs contrary to what most people today think about life, including people in the church. It was said in a sermon preached on August 12, 1849, by the famous British preacher F.W. Robertson.

> Life, like war, is a series of mistakes, and he is not the best Christian nor the best general who makes the fewest false steps. Poor mediocrity may secure that; but he is the best who wins the most splendid victories by the retrieval of mistakes. Forget mistakes; organize victories out of mistakes.[1]

Henry Ford would have agreed with Robertson, because Ford defined a mistake as "an opportunity to begin again, more intelligently." Joshua would also have agreed, because he is about to "begin again, more intelligently" and organize a victory out of his mistakes.

1. A new beginning (Josh. 8:1-2)
Once the nation of Israel had judged the sin that had defiled their camp, God was free to speak to them in mercy and

direct them in their conquest of the land. "The steps of a good man are ordered by the Lord, and He delights in his way. Though he fall, he shall not be utterly cast down; for the Lord upholds him with His hand" (Ps. 37:23-24, NKJV). No matter what mistakes we may make, the worst mistake of all is not to try again; for "the victorious Christian life is a series of new beginnings" (Alexander Whyte).

You start with the Word of God. We today don't hear God's audible voice as people often did in Bible times, but we have the Word of God before us and the Spirit of God within us; and God will direct us if we wait patiently before Him.

The word of encouragement (Josh. 8:1a). Discouragement over the past and fear of the future are the two reactions that often accompany failure. We look back and remember the mistakes that we made, and then we look ahead and wonder whether there's any future for people who fail so foolishly.

The answer to our discouragement and fear is in *hearing and believing* God's Word: "Fear not, neither be thou dismayed" (v. 1). I recommend that you take your Bible concordance and study the "fear not" statements of the Bible. Note that God spoke these words to different kinds of people in various circumstances, and His Word always met the need. Be sure to check the "fear not" statements in Genesis, Isaiah 41–44, and the first eight chapters of Luke. *God never discourages His people from making progress.* As long as we obey His commandments, we have the privilege of claiming His promises. God delights "to show Himself strong in the behalf of them whose heart is perfect [wholly devoted] toward Him" (2 Chron. 16:9).

The word of instruction (Josh. 8:1b-2). God always has a plan for His people to follow, and the only way for us to have victory is to obey God's instructions. In his first attack on Ai Joshua followed the advice of his spies and used only part of the army; but God told him to take "all the people of war"

(v. 1). The Lord also told Joshua to use an ambush and take advantage of Ai's self-confidence stemming from Israel's first defeat (7:1-5). Finally, God gave the soldiers the right to claim the spoils, but they were to burn the city. Had Achan waited only a few days, he could have picked up all the wealth that he wanted. *God always gives His best to those who leave the choice with Him.* When we run ahead of the Lord, we usually rob ourselves and hurt others.

The word of promise (Josh. 8:1c). "I have given" was God's promise (see 6:2) and Joshua's guarantee of victory as long as he obeyed the instructions of the Lord. "God never made a promise that was too good to be true," said evangelist D.L. Moody; but every promise must be claimed by faith. Unless the promises of God are "mixed with faith" (Heb. 4:2), they accomplish nothing. Because Israel acted presumptuously in their first attack against Ai, they failed miserably. The promises of God make the difference between faith and presumption.

You can never exaggerate the importance of the Christian soldier spending time daily in the Word of God. Unless daily we take the sword of the Spirit by faith (Eph. 6:17), we go into the battle unarmed and therefore unprepared. Spiritually minded believers are victorious because they allow the Word of God to "saturate" their minds and hearts. The Spirit using the Word controls their desires and decisions and this is the secret of victory.

No matter how badly we have failed, we can always get up and begin again; for our God is the God of new beginnings.

2. A new strategy (Josh. 8:3-13)

God is not only the God of new beginnings, but He's also the God of *infinite variety.* Remember the words of King Arthur that I quoted in chapter 2? "And God fulfills Himself in many ways/Lest one good custom should corrupt the world." God changes His leaders lest we start trusting flesh and blood instead of trusting the Lord, and He changes His methods lest we start depending on our personal experience instead of on His divine promises.

The strategy God gave Joshua for taking Ai was almost opposite the strategy He used at Jericho. The Jericho operation involved a week of marches that were carried on openly in the daylight. The attack on Ai involved a covert night operation that prepared the way for the daylight assault. The whole army was united at Jericho, but Joshua divided the army for the attack on Ai. God performed a mighty miracle at Jericho when He caused the walls to fall down flat, but there was no such miracle at Ai. Joshua and his men simply obeyed God's instructions by setting an ambush and luring the people of Ai out of their city, and the Lord gave them the victory.

It's important that we seek God's will *for each undertaking* so that we don't depend on past victories as we plan for the future. The World War II song "We did it before/And we can do it again!" doesn't always apply to the work of the Lord. How easy is it for Christian ministries to dig their way into administrative ruts that eventually become graves, simply because the leadership fails to discern whether God wants to do something new for them. The American business leader Bruce Barton (1886–1967) said, "When you're through changing, you're through."

The strategy for Ai was based on Israel's previous defeat; for God was organizing victory out of Joshua's mistakes. The people of Ai were overconfident because they had defeated Israel at the first attack, and this overconfidence would be their undoing. "We did it before, and we can do it again!"

At night Joshua and his army marched fifteen miles from Gilgal to Ai; and, using 30,000 soldiers, Joshua set up an ambush behind the city from the west (vv. 3-9). He put another 5,000 men between Ai and Bethel, which was about two miles away (v. 12). This detachment would make sure that the army from Bethel wouldn't make a surprise attack from the northwest and open another "front." The rocky terrain in the highlands around Ai made it easy for Joshua to conceal his soldiers, and the whole operation was done at night.

The plan was simple but effective. Leading the rest of the Jewish army, Joshua would make a frontal attack on Ai from the north. His men would flee as they had done the first time and by fleeing draw the self-confident people of Ai away from the protection of their city. At Joshua's signal the soldiers lying in ambush would enter the city and set it on fire. The people of Ai would be caught between two armies, and the third army would deal with any assistance that might come from Bethel.

Being a good general, Joshua lodged with his army (v. 9). He certainly encouraged them to trust the Lord and believe His promise for victory. The Captain of the host of the Lord (5:14) would go before them because they obeyed His Word and trusted His promises.

The work of the Lord requires strategy, and Christian leaders must seek the mind of the Lord in their planning. Like Joshua, we must get the facts and weigh them carefully as we seek the will of God. Too often, the work of the Lord only drifts along on the tide of time, without any rudder or compass to give direction; and the results are disappointing. Our English word *strategy* comes from two Greek words that together mean "to lead an army." Leadership demands planning, and planning is an important part of strategy.

3. A new victory (Josh. 8:14-29)

Ai emptied (Josh. 8:14-17). When morning dawned, the king of Ai saw the army of Israel positioned before the city, ready to attack. Confident of victory, he led his men out of the city and against the Jews. "They are the most in danger," said Matthew Henry, "who are least aware of it." Joshua and his men began to flee, and this gave the men of Ai even more assurance of victory.

According to verse 17, the men of Bethel were also involved in the attack; but no details are given. Whether they were already in Ai or arrived on the scene just in time, we aren't told; but their participation led to the defeat of their city (12:16) as well as Ai.

It was careless of the people of Ai to leave their city undefended, but such are the follies of self-confidence. When a small army sees a large army flee without even fighting, it gives them a feeling of superiority that can lead to defeat.

Ai captured (Josh. 8:18-20). Conscious that the battle was the Lord's (1 Sam. 17:47; 2 Chron. 20:15), Joshua waited for further instructions. God then told him to lift up his spear toward the city (Josh. 8:18). This was the signal for the other troops to enter the city and burn it, but the signal had to be given at just the right time. The men of Ai and Bethel were trapped, and it was a simple matter for the army of Israel to destroy them. Joshua held up his spear until the victory was won (v. 26), an action that reminds us of the battle Joshua fought against Amalek when Moses held up his hands to the Lord (Ex. 17:8-16).

Ai's army and people destroyed (Josh. 8:21-29). Seeing the smoke of the city, Joshua's men stopped fleeing, and they turned and attacked the army of Ai that was pursuing them. After the Jewish soldiers in Ai left the city, they joined in the battle. The enemy was then caught between two armies. "Israel cut them down, leaving them neither survivors nor fugitives" (v. 22, NIV).

Once the army was annihilated, the rest of the population of the city was destroyed, just as at Jericho (vv. 24-25; 6:21, 24). Keep in mind that this was not the "slaughter of innocent people" but the judgment of God on an evil society that had long resisted His grace and truth.

Ai's king slain (Josh. 8:23, 29). This was the final symbolic gesture of complete victory on the part of Israel. The king had no army, subjects, or city; for the Lord had destroyed them all. It was total victory on the part of Israel. Joshua killed the king with a sword and then ordered that the corpse be humiliated by hanging it on a tree until sundown (Deut. 21:22-23). The body was then buried under a heap of stones at the entrance of the gate of the ruin that had once been Ai. The previous heap of stones that Israel had raised was a memorial to Achan who had caused their defeat at Ai (Josh. 7:25-26). But this heap of stones at Ai was a memorial of Israel's victory over the enemy. By obeying the Word of the Lord, they had organized victory out of mistakes.

Ai's spoils claimed (Josh. 8:27). Since the firstfruits of the spoils of war in Canaan had already been given to God at Jericho, He permitted the army to claim the spoils at Ai. Furthermore, at Jericho, the victory was theirs because of a miracle of God; while at Ai, because the men actually had to fight, they earned their reward. (For the laws governing the distribution of spoils, see Num. 31:19-54.) We aren't sure that these rules were strictly followed in every situation, but they give you an indication of how Israel handled the spoils of war.

When at the close of the day the men buried the king of Ai under a heap of stones, there must have been a new sense of faith and courage in Israel; for they had won another victory. The people saw that not one word of God's promise had failed. The disgrace and defeat caused by Achan had now been erased, and Israel was well on her way to conquering the Promised Land.

4. A new commitment (Josh. 8:30-35)

At some time following the victory at Ai, Joshua led the people thirty miles north to Shechem, which lies in the valley between Mt. Ebal and Mt. Gerizim. Here the nation obeyed what Moses had commanded them to do in his farewell speech (Deut. 27:1-8). Joshua interrupted the military activities to give Israel the opportunity to make a new commitment to the authority of Jehovah as expressed in His law.

Joshua built an altar (Josh. 8:30-31). Since Abraham had built an altar at Shechem (Gen. 12:6-7), and Jacob had lived there a short time (chap. 33–34), the area had strong historic ties to Israel. Joshua's altar was built on Mt. Ebal, "the mount of cursing," because only a sacrifice of blood can save sinners from the curse of the law (Gal. 3:10-14).

In building the altar, Joshua was careful to obey Exodus 20:25 and not apply any tool to the stones picked up in the field. No human work was to be associated with the sacrifice lest sinners think their own works can save them (Eph. 2:8-9). God asked for a simple stone altar, not one that was designed and decorated by human hands, "that no flesh should glory in His presence" (1 Cor. 1:29). It's not the beauty of man-made religion that gives the sinner forgiveness, but the blood on the altar (Lev. 17:11). King Ahab replaced God's altar with a pagan altar, but it didn't give him acceptance with God or make him a better man (2 Kings 16:9-16).

The priests offered burnt offerings to the Lord as a token of the nation's total commitment to Him (Lev. 1). The peace offerings, or "fellowship offerings," were an expression of gratitude to God for His goodness (3; 7:11-34). A portion of the meat was given to the priests and another portion to the offerer so that he could eat it joyfully with his family in the presence of the Lord (7:15-16, 30-34; Deut. 12:17-18). By these sacrifices, the nation of Israel was assuring God of their commitment to Him and their fellowship with Him.

Joshua wrote the Law on stones (Josh 8:32-33). This act was in obedience to the command of Moses (Deut. 27:1-8). In the

Near East of that day it was customary for kings to celebrate their greatness by writing records of their military exploits on huge stones covered with plaster. But the secret of Israel's victory was not their leader or their army; it was their obedience to God's Law (Josh. 1:7-8). In later years, whenever Israel turned away from God's Law, they got into trouble and had to be disciplined. "And what great nation is there that has such statutes and righteous judgments as are in all this Law which I set before you this day?" asked Moses (Deut. 4:8, NKJV).

Believers today have the Word of God written on their hearts by the Holy Spirit of God (Rom. 8:1-4; 2 Cor. 3). The Law written on stones was external, not internal, and could instruct the people but could never change them. Paul makes it clear in the Epistle to the Galatians that while the Law can convict sinners and bring them to Christ (Gal. 3:19-25), it can never convert sinners and make them like Christ. Only the Spirit of God can do that.

This is now the fourth public monument of stones that has been erected. The first was at Gilgal (Josh. 4:20), commemorating Israel's passage across the Jordan. The second was in the Valley of Achor, a monument to Achan's sin and God's judgment (7:26). The third was at the entrance to Ai, a reminder of God's faithfulness to help His people (8:29). These stones on Mt. Ebal reminded Israel that their success lie only in their obedience to God's Law (1:7-8).

Joshua read the Law (Josh. 8:34-35). The tribes were assigned their places in front of the two mounts, according to Moses' instructions in Deuteronomy 27:11-13. Reuben, Gad, Asher, Zebulun, Dan, and Naphtali were at Mt. Ebal, the mount of cursing; and Simeon, Levi, Judah, Issachar, Joseph (Ephraim and Manasseh), and Benjamin were at Mt. Gerizim, the mount of blessing. The tribes at Mt. Gerizim were founded by men who had either Leah or Rachel for their mother, while the tribes at Mt. Ebal were descended from either Zilpah or Bilhah, handmaids of Leah and Rachel. The only exceptions were Reuben and Zebulun, who belonged to Leah. Reuben had forfeited his status as the firstborn because he had sinned against his father (Gen. 35:22; 49:3-4).

In the valley between the two mountains stood the priests and Levites with the ark, surrounded by the elders, officers, and judges of the nation. The people were all facing the ark, which represented the presence of the Lord among His people. When Joshua and the Levites read the blessings of the Lord one by one (see Deut. 28:1-14), the tribes at Mt. Gerizim responded with a loud united "Amen!" which in the Hebrew means "So be it!" When they read the curses (see Deut. 27:14-26), the tribes at Mt. Ebal would respond with their "Amen" after each curse was read.

God had given the Law through Moses *at Mt. Sinai* (Ex. 19–20), and the people had accepted it and promised to obey. Moses then repeated and explained the Law *on the Plains of Moab* at the border of Canaan. He applied that Law to their lives in the Promised Land and admonished them to obey it. "See, I am setting before you today a blessing and a curse— the blessing if you obey the commands of the Lord your God that I am giving you today; the curse if you disobey the commands of the Lord your God" (Deut. 11:26-28, NIV; note vv. 29-32).

Joshua now reaffirmed the Law *in the land of promise.* Since the area between Mt. Ebal and Mt. Gerizim was a natural amphitheater, everybody could hear the words of the Law clearly and respond with intelligence. By shouting "Amen" to the statements that were read, the people admitted that they understood the Law with its blessings and curses, and that they accepted the responsibility of obeying it. This included the women, children, and the "mixed multitude" (sojourners) who had joined Israel (Ex. 12:38; 22:21; 23:9; Deut. 24:17-22;

31:12). If they wanted to share in Israel's conquest, they had to submit to the Law of Israel's God.

God's people today stand in a valley between two mounts—Mt. Calvary, where Jesus died for our sins, and Mt. Olivet, where He will return in power and great glory (Zech. 14:4). The Old Testament prophets saw the Messiah's suffering and glory, but they did not see the "valley" between this present age of the church (1 Peter 1:10-12). Believers today aren't living under the curse of the Law, because Jesus bore that curse "on a tree" (Gal. 3:10-14). In Christ believers are blessed with "every spiritual blessing" (Eph. 1:3, NKJV) because of the grace of God. For them life means the blessings of Gerizim and not the curses of Ebal.

However, because Christians "are not under the Law, but under grace" (Rom. 6:14; 7:1-6), it doesn't mean that we can live any way we please and ignore the Law of God or defy it. We aren't saved by keeping the Law, nor are we sanctified by trying to meet the demands of the Law; but "the righteousness of the Law" is "fulfilled in us" as we walk in the power of the Holy Spirit (Rom. 8:4). If we put ourselves under Law, we forfeit the enjoyment of the blessings of grace (Gal. 5). If we walk in the Spirit, we experience His life-changing power and live so as to please God.

Let's give thanks that Jesus bore the curse of the Law for us on the cross and that He bestows all the blessings of the heavenlies on us through the Spirit. By faith we can claim our inheritance in Christ and march forth in victory!

Notes
1. Frederick W. Robertson, *Sermons Preached at Brighton, First Series* (London: Kegan Paul, Trench, Trubner and Co., 1898), p. 66.

We Have Met the Enemy and He Is Our Neighbor

An anonymous wit reminds us that a dentist's mistake is pulled out, a lawyer's mistake is imprisoned, a teacher's mistake is failed, a printer's mistake is corrected, a pharmacist's mistake is buried, a postman's mistake is forwarded, and an electrician's mistake could be shocking. The novelist Joseph Conrad wrote, "It's only those who do nothing that make no mistakes."

In Joshua's case, however, doing nothing *was* his mistake; and this chapter explains what happened. It records the three stages in his second failure (after Ai) in the conquest of the Promised Land. It also tells us how Joshua turned his mistake into a victory.

1. Believing the enemy (Josh. 9:1-15)

While Israel was at Mt. Ebal and Mt. Gerizim, reaffirming their commitment to the Lord, the kings in Canaan were getting ready to attack. They had heard about the defeat of Jericho and Ai and were not about to give up without a fight. It was time for them to go on the offensive and attack these Jewish invaders. The city-states in Canaan were not always friendly with one another, but local rivals can often come together when they have a common enemy (Ps. 2:1-2; Luke 23:12).

After an experience of great blessing, God's people must be especially prepared to confront the enemy; for like Canaan, the Christian life is "a land of hills and valleys" (Deut. 11:11). But Israel's greatest danger wasn't the confederation of the armies of Canaan. It was a group of men from Gibeon who were about to enter the camp and deceive Joshua and the princes of Israel. Satan sometimes comes as a devouring lion (1 Peter 5:8) and sometimes as a deceiving serpent (2 Cor. 11:3), and we must be alert and protected by the spiritual armor God has provided for us (Eph. 6:10-18).

What the Gibeonites did (Josh. 9:3-5). Gibeon was located only twenty-five miles from the camp of Israel at Gilgal and was on Joshua's list to be destroyed. In Deuteronomy 20:10-20, God's law stated that Israel must destroy all the cities in Canaan. If after the Conquest Israel was involved in other wars, they could offer peace to cities that were outside the land. (See also 7:1-11.) Somehow the Gibeonites knew about this law and decided to use it for their own protection. Since the enemy knows how to use the Word of God for their own purposes, God's people must keep alert (Matt. 4:5-7).

The Gibeonites assembled a group of men and equipped them to look like an official delegation from a foreign city. Their clothing, food, and equipment were all designed to give the impression that they had been on a long and difficult journey from a distant city. Satan is a counterfeiter and "masquerades as an angel of light" (2 Cor. 11:14, NIV). He has his "false apostles" and "deceitful workmen" (v. 13, NIV) at work in this world, blinding the lost and seeking to lead believers astray. It's much easier for us to identify the lion when he's roaring than to detect the serpent when he's slithering into our lives.

What the Gibeonites said (Josh. 9:6-13). Satan is a liar and the father of lies (John 8:44), and human nature is such that many people find it easier to tell lies than the truth. With tongue in cheek, the American political leader Adlai Stevenson said, "A lie is an abomination unto the Lord—and a very present help in trouble." The Gibeonites told several lies in their attempt to get out of trouble.

First, they said they were "from a very far country" (Josh. 9:6, 9) when they actually lived twenty-five miles away. Then they lied about their clothing and food. "This bread of ours was warm when we packed it at home on the day we left to come to you. But now see how dry and moldy it is" (v. 12, NIV). They also lied about themselves and gave the impression that they were important envoys on an official peace mission from the elders of their city. They also called themselves "your servants" (vv. 8, 9, 11), when in reality they were the enemies of Israel.

These four lies were bad enough; but when the visitors said they had come "because of the name of the Lord" (v. 9), it was blasphemous. Like the citizens of Jericho (2:10), the people in Gibeon had heard about Israel's march of conquest (9:9-10); but unlike Rahab and her family, they didn't put their faith in the Lord. These men were wise enough not to mention Israel's victories at Jericho and Ai; for that news couldn't have reached their "far country" that quickly. Satan's ambassadors can lie more convincingly than some Christians can tell the truth!

Satan knows how to use "religious lies" to give the impression that people are seeking to know the Lord. In my pastoral ministry I've met people who have introduced themselves as *seekers;* but the longer they talked, the more convinced I was that they were *sneakers,* trying to get something out of me and the church. They would make their "profession of faith" and then start telling me their sad tale of woe, hoping to break my heart and then pick my pocket. Of all liars, "religious liars" are the worst. If you need to be convinced of this, read 2 Peter 2 and the Epistle of Jude.

Why they succeeded (Josh. 9:14-15). The reason is simple: Joshua and the princes of Israel were impetuous and didn't take time to consult the Lord. They walked by sight and not by faith. After listening to the strangers' speech and examining the evidence, Joshua and his leaders concluded that the men were telling the truth. The leaders of Israel took the "scientific approach" instead of the "spiritual approach." They depended on their own senses, examined the "facts," discussed the matter, and agreed in their conclusion. It was all very logical and convincing, but it was all wrong. They had made the same mistake at Ai (chap. 7) and hadn't yet learned to wait on the Lord and seek His direction.

The will of God comes from the heart of God (Ps. 33:11), and He delights to make it known to His children *when He knows they are humble and willing to obey.* We don't seek God's will like customers who look at options but like servants who listen for orders. "If any of you really determines to do God's will, then you will certainly know" (John 7:17, TLB) is a basic principle for victorious Christian living. God sees our hearts and knows whether we are really serious about obeying Him. Certainly we ought to use the mind God has given us, but we must heed the warning of Proverbs 3:5-6 and not *lean on* our own understanding.

If this group of men had been an authentic official delegation, it would have comprised a much larger company bearing adequate supplies, including sufficient provisions for the trip home. Real ambassadors would have thrown away their "dry and moldy" bread because their servants would have baked fresh bread for them. As officials, they would have packed the proper attire so that they might make the best impression possible as they negotiated with the enemy. Had Joshua and his leaders paused to think and pray about what they saw, they would have concluded that the whole thing was a trick. "If any of you lacks wisdom, let him ask of God, who gives to all liberally and without reproach, and it will be given to him" (James 1:5, NKJV).

True faith involves exercising patience (Heb. 6:12). "Whoever believes will not act hastily" (Isa. 28:16, NKJV). Moses had told the Jews, "Be careful not to make a treaty with those who live in the land where you are going, or they will be a snare among you" (Ex. 34:12, NIV). But in their haste Joshua and the Jewish leaders broke God's Law and made a covenant with the enemy. Since their oath was sworn in the name of the Lord (Josh. 9:18), it could not be broken. Joshua and the princes of Israel had sworn to their own hurt (Ps. 15:4; Ecc. 5:1-7), and there was no way to revoke their oath or be released from their promise.

Like Joshua and the nation of Israel, God's people today are living in enemy territory and must constantly exercise caution. When you believe the enemy instead of seeking the mind of the Lord, you can expect to get into trouble.

2. Enlisting the enemy (Josh 9:16-27)

How did the leaders of Israel discover that they had made a big mistake? Knowing that they were now out of danger, perhaps the "ambassadors" openly admitted what they had done. Or maybe the Gibeonites were overheard rejoicing in their success. Did some of Joshua's spies return to camp after reconnaissance and recognize the enemy? Perhaps the Gibeonites overheard the plans for Israel's next attack and had to inform the leaders that a solemn oath now protected those cities. However it happened, Joshua discovered that he and the princes had blundered; and no doubt they were humbled and embarrassed because of it.

We must give the leaders credit for being men of their word. To violate their oath would have been to take the holy name of Jehovah in vain, and this would have brought about divine judgment. Years later King Saul violated this oath; and God judged the nation severely (2 Sam. 21). Military leaders of lesser character than Joshua might have argued that "all's fair in love and war" and forced the Gibeonites to divulge information that would help him conquer their city. Instead, when the Jewish army arrived at Gibeon and the neighboring cities, they didn't attack them.

Why did the Jewish people grumble at what their leaders had done? Because this covenant with Gibeon would cost the soldiers dearly in plunder they would never get from the protected cities. Furthermore, the Gibeonites and their neighbors might influence the Jews with their pagan practices and lead them away from the Lord. Moses had given Israel stern warnings against compromising with the people of the land (Deut. 7), and now they had foolishly made a covenant with the enemy. However, we wonder what decisions the common people would have made had they been in the place of the leaders. It's easy to criticize after the fact!

But that wasn't the end of the story. Joshua and his associates teach us an important lesson: If you make a mistake, admit it; *and then make your mistake work for you!* The leaders put the Gibeonites to work hauling water and fuel for the service of the tabernacle, where both water and wood were used in abundance. In later years the Gibeonites were called *the Nethinim* ("given ones" = given to assist the priests) and labored as servants in the temple (1 Chron. 9:2; Ezra 2:43, 58; Neh. 3:26). In Joshua 10, we shall see that God overruled Joshua's mistake and used it to give him a signal victory over five kings at one time.

Of course, the Gibeonites would rather submit to humiliating service than be destroyed as were the inhabitants of Jericho and Ai. There's no evidence in Scripture that the descendants of the Gibeonites created any problems for the Jews.

It's likely that their service in the tabernacle, and later in the temple, influenced them to abandon their idols and worship the God of Israel. The fact that over 500 hundred Nephilim returned to Jerusalem after the Babylonian Captivity (Ezra 2:43-58; 8:20) suggests that they were devoted to the Lord and His house.

3. Defending the enemy (Josh. 10:1-28)

When you make agreements with the enemy, expect to end up paying a price and having to defend them in order to protect yourself. This is why God's people must remain separated from the world (2 Cor. 6:14-18). I wonder whether Paul had Joshua in mind when he wrote, "No one engaged in warfare entangles himself with the affairs of this life, that he may please Him who enlisted him as a soldier" (2 Tim. 2:4, NKJV).

The king's call to the armies (Josh. 10:1-5). The king of Jerusalem, whose name means "lord of righteousness," heard what the Gibeonites had done and announced that these traitors had to be punished. If a great city like Gibeon capitulated to the Jews, then one more barrier was removed against the advancement of Israel in the land. It was important for the Canaanites to recover that key city, even if they had to take it by force. Four other Canaanite kings allied with Adoni-zedek, and their combined armies encamped before Gibeon. The poor Gibeonites had made peace with the invaders and were now at war with their former allies!

As this confederation of armies and kings assembled, God in heaven must have laughed (Ps. 2:1-4), because unknown to them He was using these events to accomplish His own purposes. *Instead of having to defeat these five city-states one by one, He would help Joshua conquer them all at one time!* Just as God used the defeat at Ai to form a battle plan for victory over Ai (Josh. 8), so also He used Joshua's mistake with the

Gibeonites to protect Gibeon and accelerate the conquest of Canaan.

The mistakes we make embarrass us, especially those mistakes that are caused by our running ahead of the Lord and not seeking His will. But we need to remember that no mistake is final for the dedicated Christian. God can use even our blunders to accomplish His purposes. Somebody defined success as "the art of making your mistakes when nobody's looking"; but a better definition would be "the art of seeing victory where other people see only defeat."

The Gibeonites' call to Joshua (Josh. 10:6-7). In spite of their paganism, these Gibeonites are a good example for people to follow today. When they knew they were headed for destruction, they came to Joshua ("Jehovah is Savior") and obtained from him a promise of protection. Would that lost sinners realize their plight and turn to Jesus Christ by faith! When the Gibeonites found themselves in danger, they believed Joshua's promise and called on him for help. That's what God's people need to do when they find themselves facing the battles of life. The Gibeonites turned the whole burden over to Joshua and trusted him to keep his word, and he did.

Joshua's call to the Lord (Josh. 10:8-15). Three factors combined to give Joshua success in this attack: believing a divine promise (v. 8), using sound strategy (v. 9), and calling on the Lord in prayer (vv. 10-15).

The promise. Joshua's actions here illustrate two important verses: "Whatsoever is not of faith is sin" (Rom. 14:23) and "faith cometh by hearing, and hearing by the word of God" (10:17). Whenever we believe the promises of God and obey the commands of God, we act by faith and can expect God's help. The Jews didn't have to be afraid because God had already promised them victory. God's promises of victory had encouraged Joshua when he became leader of the nation (Josh. 1:5-9), when he anticipated attacking Jericho (6:2), and

113

when he attacked Ai after a humiliating defeat (8:1). God's promises would be fulfilled because "there has not failed one word of all His good promise" (1 Kings 8:56, NKJV).

The strategy. But faith apart from works is dead, and Joshua proved his faith by using wise strategy. He ordered an all-night march and a surprise attack on the enemy army, strategy he had used before when attacking Ai (8:3ff). It was a long trek from Gilgal to Gibeon, and the road was uphill; but Joshua assembled his troops and made the journey as quickly as possible. No doubt the men were weary when they arrived, but the Lord was with them and gave them victory. What kept the soldiers going? They believed God's promise and knew that the victory was assured.

God assisted the weary Jewish soldiers by killing the enemy army with large hailstones. The timely occurrence of the storm was itself a miracle, but an even greater miracle was the fact that the stones *hit only the enemy soldiers.* God took His special "ammunition" out of His storehouse and used it to good advantage (Job 38:22-23). When God's people are obeying God's will, everything in the universe works for them, even "the stars in their courses" (Jud. 5:20). When we disobey God's will, everything works against us. (Read Jonah 1 for a vivid illustration of this truth.)

The prayer. But the miracle of the hailstorm was nothing compared to the miracle of extending the day so that Joshua could finish the battle and secure a complete victory over the enemy. His men were weary and the task was great; and if night came on, the enemy could escape. Joshua needed a special act from God to enable him to claim the victory the Lord had promised.

This is the last miracle recorded in Joshua and certainly the greatest. Joshua prayed for God's help, and the Lord answered in a remarkable way. This event is questioned by those who deny the reality of miracles and look only to science for truth. "How could God stop the rotation of the earth and extend the length of a day," they ask, "without creating chaos all over the planet?" They seem to forget the fact that days are *normally* of different lengths in various parts of the world without the planet experiencing chaos. At 2 o'clock in the morning, I read the newspaper *by sunlight* in Norway.

But how do you explain a miracle, *any* miracle? Of course, the simplest answer is the answer of faith: The Lord is God and nothing is too hard for Him (Jer. 32:17, 27). Day and night belong to God (Ps. 74:16), and everything He has made is His servant. If God can't perform the miracle described in Joshua 10, then He can't perform *any* miracle and is imprisoned in His own creation, unable to use or suspend the very laws He built into it. I have a difficult time believing in that kind of a God.

An Old Testament expert, Gleason L. Archer, points out that the phrase "hasted not to go down" in verse 13 indicates "a retardation of the movement" and not a complete cessation.[1] The sun and moon didn't stand still permanently and then suddenly go down but were held back so that the daylight was lengthened. God stopped the sun and moon and then retarded the rotation of the planet so that the sun and moon set very slowly. Such a process would not create chaos all over the globe.

A corollary to this view is that the sun and moon remained on their normal course and it only *appeared* that the day was lengthening because of the way God caused their light to be refracted. But verse 13 states twice that the sun "stood still" and once that the moon "stayed." However, these verbs need not describe a permanent situation but only the beginning of the miracle. God stopped the sun and moon in their courses and then controlled their gradual descent, all the while causing the light to be refracted for a much longer period of time.

Since verses 13b-15 are poetical in form, a quotation from

the unknown Book of Jasher (see 2 Sam. 1:8), some students interpret the words symbolically. They say that God so helped Israel that the army was able to accomplish two days' work in one day. But Joshua's words sound very much like a prayer that the Lord would intervene, and the description of what occurred doesn't read like the report of an efficiency expert.

Why try to explain away a miracle? What do we prove? Certainly not that we're smarter than God! Either we believe in a God who can do anything, or we must accept a Christian faith that's nonmiraculous; and that does away with the inspiration of the Bible, the Virgin Birth, and the bodily resurrection of Jesus Christ. Certainly there's room for honest questions about the *nature* of the miraculous; but for the humble Christian believer, there's never room for questioning the *reality* of the miraculous. C.S. Lewis wrote, "The mind which asks for a nonmiraculous Christianity is a mind in process of relapsing from Christianity into mere 'religion.' "[2]

You find seemingly contradictory facts stated in Joshua 10:15 and 21. Why would the army go all the way back to Gilgal when the battle wasn't over? The best explanation is to see verse 15 as the completion of the quotation from the Book of Jasher, beginning at verse 13b. The temporary Jewish camp was at Makkedah, which was near Libnah; and the army didn't return to Gilgal until they had established their control over central Canaan.

Joshua's call to his army (Josh. 10:16-28). At the end of an incredible battle, Joshua performed a public ceremony that gave encouragement and strength to his soldiers. Their past victories had given them control over the central part of the land, but now they faced campaigns in both the south and the north of Palestine. "Divide and conquer" was Joshua's strategy, and it worked. Joshua wanted to remind his men that the Lord would give them victory throughout the land.

Knowing that the five kings were trapped in a cave, Joshua temporarily left them and led his men in the "mopping up" operation, which verse 20 describes as "slaying them with a very great slaughter." Only a few of the enemy soldiers escaped to the cities; but since those cities would eventually be destroyed anyway, those fugitives had no hope.

Returning to the camp, probably the next day, Joshua ordered the kings to be taken from the cave and put on the ground, their faces in the dirt. This humiliating posture announced that Joshua had won a total victory and their end had come. But there was more. He called for his officers to put their feet on the necks of the kings, symbolic not only of the past victory but also of the victories the Lord would give His people in the days ahead. The kings were slain and the five corpses hung on five trees until sundown. Then their bodies were put into the cave, with a pile of stones closing up the entrance. This pile of stones was another monument in the land speaking of the power and victory of the Lord.

In verse 25, Joshua's words must have thrilled the hearts of his brave soldiers. They echo the words God spoke to him when he began his career (1:6-9). Since Joshua is a type of Jesus Christ, we can apply this scene and these words to Christ and His people. Jesus has defeated all His enemies and will one day return and destroy them forever. No matter how they may rage and rebel (Ps. 2:1-3), our Lord's enemies are only the footstool at His feet (Ps. 110:1; 1 Cor. 15:25). Through Him, we can claim victory and put our feet on the necks of our enemies (Rom. 16:20).

As you review the whole episode of Joshua and the Gibeonites, you can't help but be both warned and encouraged. These events warn us to be alert and prayerful lest the enemy deceive us and we start walking by sight instead of by faith. Then we'll find ourselves making decisions that are wrong and getting into alliances that are dangerous. But there's also a word of encouragement: God can take even our blunders and turn them into blessings. This isn't an excuse for carelessness, but it is a great encouragement when you've failed the Lord and His people.

"And this is the victory that has overcome the world—our faith" (1 John 5:4, NKJV).

Notes

1. See *Encyclopedia of Bible Difficulties,* by Gleason L. Archer (Grand Rapids: Zondervan, 1982), pp. 161–62.

2. C.S. Lewis, *Miracles* (New York: Macmillan, 1960), p. 133.

INTERLUDE

This section of the Book of Joshua summarizes Israel's conquest of the southern (10:29-43) and northern cities (11:1-15) in Palestine, and closes with a list of the names of some of the kings whom Israel defeated (11:16–12:24). Since there is probably a map of the Conquest located in the back of your Bible, consult it as you read these chapters.

Two things stand out in this record: It was the Lord who gave the victory (10:30, 32, 42; 11:6, 8); and Joshua obeyed the Lord by utterly destroying the enemy, just as Moses had commanded (11:9, 12, 15, 20). The only exception was Gibeon.

Joshua's strategy was to cut across the land and divide it, then conquer the southern cities, then the northern cities. On more than one occasion, he made a surprise attack on the enemy (10:9; 11:7); and the promises of the Lord encouraged him (v. 6; see 1:9; 8:1).

In 10:29-35, you have the record of the army fighting in the foothills; but in verse 36, the campaign moves to the mountains. The northern coalition of kings was unable to defeat Israel even though their army was much larger than that of the Jews (11:1-9).

The "long time" of verse 18 is about seven years. Israel's failure at Kadesh Barnea (Deut. 2:14), at which time Caleb was forty years old (Josh. 14:7) to their crossing of the Jordan was thirty-eight years. He was eighty-five when the Conquest was over (v. 10), which means that at least seven years had been devoted to the campaign.

The Anakim mentioned in 11:21-22 were a race of giants,

descendants of Anak, who were greatly feared by the ten unbelieving men who had spied out Canaan (Num. 13:22, 28, 33). The two believing spies, Joshua and Caleb, didn't fear them but had trusted the Lord for victory. Joshua's victory over the Anakim is recorded in Joshua 11:21-22 and Caleb's victory in 14:12-15.

The apparent contradiction between verses 11:23 and 13:1 can easily be explained. Joshua and his army did take control of the whole land by destroying the key cities with their kings and people. Israel didn't take every little city or slay every citizen or ruler, but they did enough to break the power of the enemy and establish control over the land. Once this was accomplished and there was rest in the land, Joshua was able to assign each tribe its inheritance; and within each inheritance, the tribes had to gain mastery over the remaining inhabitants who were still there. Even after the death of Joshua and his officers, there was additional land to be taken (Jud. 1–3).

Thirty-three kings are named in Joshua 12, beginning with Sihon and Og whose lands were east of Jordan and had been conquered under the leadership of Moses (vv. 1-8; Num. 21:21-35). The sixteen kings defeated in the southern campaign are listed in Joshua 12:9-16 and the fifteen northern kings in verses 17-24.

Now we turn to the actual assigning of the land to the tribes (chaps. 13–21) to discover the spiritual truths we need to learn and apply as we claim our own spiritual inheritance in Jesus Christ.

This Land Is Our Land!

Joshua had successfully completed the first half of his divine commission: He had conquered the enemy and was in control of the land and the cities (1:1-5). Now he had to fulfill the second part of that commission and divide the land so that each tribe could claim its inheritance and enjoy what God had given them (v. 6). (See Num. 34–35.)

The word *inheritance* is found over fifty times in these nine chapters and is a very important word. The Jews *inherited* their land. They didn't *win* their land as spoils of battle or *purchase* their land as in a business transaction. The Lord, who was the sole owner, leased the land to them. "The land must not be sold permanently," the Lord had instructed them, "because the land is Mine and you are but aliens and My tenants" (Lev. 25:23, NIV). Imagine having God for your landlord!

The "rent" God required was simply Israel's obedience to His Law. As long as the Jewish people honored the Lord with their worship and obedience, He would bless them, make their land productive, and keep their nation at peace with their neighbors. When Israel agreed to the blessings and curses at Mt. Gerizim and Mt. Ebal (Josh. 8:30-35), they accepted the conditions of what is called "The Palestinian Covenant." Their *ownership* of the land was purely the gracious act of God; but their *possession* and *enjoyment* of the land depended on their submission and obedience to the Lord. (See Lev. 26 and Deut. 27–30 for the details of the Palestinian Covenant.)

The Promised Land was a gift of God's love; and if the Israelites loved the Lord, they would want to obey Him and please Him in the way they used His land (Deut. 4:37-39). Unfortunately, they eventually defied the Lord, disobeyed the Law, and defiled the land; and God had to chasten them in the land of Babylon.

There were four main stages in the distribution of the land; and in each of these stages, you will find spiritual lessons for God's people today who want to enjoy their spiritual inheritance in Christ. As you study these chapters, I suggest you consult a map of the Holy Land that shows the boundaries of the twelve tribes and the cities that are involved.

1. The assignments made at Gilgal (Josh. 13:1–17:18)
Throughout the conquest of Canaan, Gilgal had been the center of operations for Israel. Later, Joshua moved the camp and the tabernacle to a more central location at Shiloh (18:1).

We don't know Joshua's exact age at this time in Israel's history, although he could well have been 100. Caleb was 85 (14:10), and it's likely that Joshua was the older of the two. Joshua lived to be 110 (24:19), and the events described in the last half of the book could well have taken over ten years.

The system for assigning the territories in Canaan is given in 14:1-2. Eleazer the high priest, Joshua, and one representative from each of the tribes (Num. 34:13-29) cast lots before the Lord and in this way determined His will (Prov. 16:33). When Joshua relocated the camp at Shiloh, they changed the system (Josh. 18:1-7).

THIS LAND IS OUR LAND!

The 2½ tribes east of the Jordan (Josh. 13:1-33). Reuben, Gad, and the half tribe of Manasseh had agreed to help the other tribes conquer the land before they returned to the east side of the Jordan to enjoy their inheritance (Num. 32). They had asked for this land outside the boundaries of Canaan because it was especially suited to the raising of cattle. The fact that these two and a half tribes would not be living within God's appointed land didn't seem to worry them. Moses graciously agreed to their choice and let them settle across the Jordan. When we study the twenty-second chapter of Joshua, we'll learn that while their choice may have been good for their cattle, it created serious problems for their children.

These tribes became a sort of "buffer zone" between the Jews in Canaan and the heathen nations like Moab and Ammon. Of course, their location made them extremely vulnerable both to military attack and ungodly influence; and both of these liabilities eventually brought about their downfall (1 Chron. 5:25-26).The boundaries are given for Reuben in the south (Josh. 13:15-23), and the half tribe of Manasseh in the north (vv. 29-32), with Gad sandwiched between (vv. 24-28).

> **Lesson #1.** Don't become a "borderline believer." Enter into the inheritance God appoints for you and rejoice in it. "He will choose our inheritance for us, the excellence of Jacob whom He loves" (Ps. 47:4, NKJV). The will of God is the expression of the love of God and is always the best for us.

Since the tribe of Reuben had taken its territory from Moab, it was logical for the story of Balaam to be mentioned here (Josh. 13:22-23; see Num. 22–25). When Balaam saw that God was turning his curses into blessings, he advised Balak to be friendly to the Jews and invite them to one of the

Moabite religious feasts. This resulted in some of the Jewish men taking Moabite women for themselves and thus violating the Law of God. What Satan couldn't accomplish as a lion, cursing Israel, he accomplished as a serpent, beguiling Israel and leading the men into wicked compromise.

Four times in these chapters, we are reminded that the Levites were given no inheritance in the land (Josh. 13:14, 33; 14:3-4; 18:7), because the Lord was their inheritance (Deut. 18:1-8; 10:8-9; Num. 18). The priests received certain portions from the sacrifices as their due, and both the priests and Levites shared in the special tithes and offerings that the people were commanded to bring.

But other factors were probably involved in scattering the tribe of Levi. For one thing, God didn't want tribal responsibilities to distract the priests and Levites; He wanted them to devote themselves fully to serving Him. (See 2 Tim. 2:4.) Also, He wanted them to be "salt and light" in the land as they lived among the people and taught them the Law. Simeon and Levi were also scattered in fulfillment of the prophecy of Jacob (Gen. 49:5-7, see chap. 34). Simeon eventually became a part of Judah.

The 2½ tribes west of the Jordan (Josh. 14:1–17:18). The next tribes to be settled were Judah in the south (14:6–15:63), Ephraim across the middle of the land (16:1-10), and the other half of Manasseh in the north (17:1-18).

Since Caleb belonged to the tribe of Judah (Num. 13:30) and had been one of the two faithful spies, he received his inheritance first. Joshua, the other faithful spy, was the last to receive his inheritance (Josh. 19:49-51). Caleb reminded his friend Joshua of the promise Moses had made to them forty-five years before (Num. 14:24, 30; Deut. 1:34-36), that they would survive the years of wandering and receive their inheritance in the land. This promise gave Joshua and Caleb joy and courage as they endured years of wandering and waiting.

Lesson #2. Be encouraged in your pilgrim journey! You have already received your inheritance in Christ and can claim "every spiritual blessing" (Eph. 1:3, NKJV). Since you have a glorious inheritance before you (1 Peter 1:3-6), keep looking up! The best is yet to come!

Caleb was eighty-five years old, but he didn't look for an easy task, suited to an "old man." He asked Joshua for mountains to climb and giants to conquer! His strength was in the Lord, and he knew that God would never fail him. The secret of Caleb's life is found in a phrase that's repeated six times in Scripture: "he wholly followed the Lord God of Israel" (Josh. 14:14; also see Num. 14:24; 32:12; Deut. 1:36; Josh. 14:8-9). Caleb was an overcomer because he had faith in the Lord (1 John 5:4).

Lesson #3. We are never too old to make new conquests of faith in the power of the Lord. Like Caleb, we can capture mountains and conquer giants if we wholly follow the Lord. No matter how old we become, we must never retire from trusting and serving the Lord.

In Joshua 15:13-19, we see Caleb providing for the next generation. Some of Caleb's daring faith rubbed off on his son-in-law Othniel, who later became a judge in the land (Jud. 3:7-11). Caleb's faith also touched his daughter, for she had the faith to ask her father for a field and then for springs of water to irrigate the land. Caleb's example of faith was more valuable to his family than the property he claimed for them.

Lesson #4. The older generation must provide for the next generation, not only materially but most of all spiritually. "Senior saints" must be examples of believers and encourage the younger generation to trust the Lord and wholly follow Him.

The inheritance of the rest of the tribe of Judah is described in Joshua 15:1-12 and 21-63. We're not sure why verse 32 says twenty-nine cities when thirty-six are named, but perhaps the names of some of the "villages" outside the city walls are included in the list. At that time the Jews couldn't take Jerusalem (v. 63). They held it temporarily later on (Jud. 1:8), and then David captured it permanently and made it the capital city (2 Sam. 5:6-10).

Ephraim and Manasseh were the sons of Joseph, whom Jacob "adopted" and especially blessed (Gen. 48:15-22). Since the tribe of Levi wasn't given any territory, these two tribes made up the difference so that there were still twelve tribes in Israel. The birth order was "Manasseh and Ephraim" (Josh. 16:4; 17:1), but Jacob reversed it. God rejects our first birth and gives us a second birth. He accepted Abel and rejected Cain; He rejected Ishmael and accepted Isaac, Abraham's second-born son; He rejected Esau and accepted Jacob.

In the nation of Israel the sons inherited the property but the daughters of Zelophehad saw to it that the daughters weren't discriminated against (vv. 3-6; Num. 27:1-11). Like the daughter of Caleb, these women had the faith and courage to ask for their inheritance; and they even changed the law!

Lesson #5. God wants to give all His people their inheritance. "You do not have because you do not ask" (James 4:2, NKJV). In Jesus Christ, all believers are one and are heirs of God (Gal. 3:26-29). Nothing from your first birth should hinder you from claiming all that you have in Jesus Christ.

Joshua had a problem with the children of Joseph (Ephraim and Manasseh), who complained because the Lord didn't give them enough room! (Josh. 17:14-18) You can detect their pride as they told Joshua what a "great people" they were. After all, didn't Jacob personally adopt and especially bless them? And hadn't they multiplied in a great way? And wasn't Joshua from the tribe of Ephraim? (Num. 13:8) They were a special people who deserved special treatment.

If you compare the statistics given in 1:32-35 and 26:34 and 37, you learn that the descendants of Joseph had increased from 72,700 to 85,200, although Ephraim had 8,000 fewer people. But six other tribes had increased their number since the last census. Thus the children of Joseph weren't the only ones who were fruitful.

Joshua told his brethren that, if they were such a great people, now was their opportunity to prove it! Let them do what Caleb did and defeat the giants and claim the mountains! It's worth noting that the people of Ephraim and Manasseh seemed to be given to criticism and pride. They not only created problems for Joshua but also for Gideon (Jud. 8:1-3), Jephthah (12:1-7), and even David (2 Sam. 20:1-5). "For where envy and self-seeking exist, confusion and every evil thing are there" (James 3:16, NKJV).

> **Lesson #6.** It's not your boasting but your believing that gives you the victory and gains you new territory. Sometimes those who talk the most accomplish the least.

2. The assignments made at Shiloh (Josh. 18:1–19:51)

Five tribes now had been given their inheritance as Joshua, Eleazer, and the twelve tribal leaders cast lots at Gilgal. Then Joshua moved the camp to Shiloh, in the territory of Ephraim, where the tabernacle remained until David moved the ark to

Jerusalem (2 Sam. 6). The Lord must have directed Joshua to make this move or he would not have done it (Deut. 12:5-7). Shiloh was centrally located and was more convenient for all the tribes.

Seven tribes still had to have their inheritance marked out for them, and apparently they were slow to respond to the challenge. Unlike Caleb and the daughters of Zelophehad, these tribes didn't have faith and spiritual zeal. These tribes had helped fight battles and defeat the enemy, but now they hesitated to claim their inheritance and enjoy the land God had given them. "The lazy man does not roast what he took in hunting, but diligence is man's precious possession" (Prov. 12:27, NKJV).

At this point, Joshua and the leaders inaugurated a new system for allocating the land. After each of the seven tribes appointed three men, all twenty-one men went through the remaining territories and listed the cities and the landmarks, describing each part of the land. They brought this information back to Joshua, who then assigned the various portions to the remaining seven tribes by casting lots before the Lord.

Since Benjamin was the full brother to Joseph, his territory was assigned adjacent to Ephraim and Manasseh (Josh. 18:11-28). Simeon shared his inheritance with Judah (19:1-9; see Gen. 49:7) and eventually inhabited the cities assigned in Joshua 15:21ff. The children of Joseph wanted more territory, but weren't willing to fight for it by faith; but the people of Judah had so much land that they shared it with Simeon. What a contrast!

The area north of Manasseh was assigned to Zebulun (19:10-16), Issachar (vv. 17-23), Asher (vv. 24-31), and Naphtali (vv. 32-39). Zebulun and Naphtali later became "Galilee of the Gentiles" (Matt. 4:15-16), where our Lord ministered when He was here on earth. The "sea of Chinneroth" (see Josh. 12:3; 13:27) is the Sea of Galilee. The Hebrew word *chinnereth* means "harp," and the Sea of Galilee is shaped like a harp.

The last tribe to receive its assignment was the tribe of Dan (19:40-48), which immediately went to work and expanded its territory. Dan and Benjamin formed a "belt" across the land, connecting the Dead Sea with the Mediterranean.

Being the leader that he was, Joshua waited until the very last to claim his own inheritance; and the Lord gave him the city of Timnath-Serah (vv. 49-50). Like his friend Caleb, Joshua preferred living in the mountainous region of the land.

3. The assignment of the cities of refuge (Josh. 20:1-9)
When the nation was still on the other side of the Jordan, God told Moses to have the people set aside special cities for the Levites (Num. 35:1-5), as well as six "cities of refuge" (Ex. 21:13; Num. 35:6-34); Deut. 19:1-13). Now that the tribes had received their territories, Joshua could assign these cities.

Even before the Law of Moses was given, God had laid down the basic rule that those who shed blood should pay for their crime with their own blood (Gen. 9:5-6). This principle was enunciated repeatedly in the Law, but God made a distinction between murder and manslaughter (Ex. 21:12-14; Lev. 24:17; Num. 35:16-21; Deut. 19:11-13). "Blood defiles the land, and no atonement can be made for the land, for the blood that is shed on it, except by the blood of him who shed it. Therefore do not defile the land which you inhabit" (Num. 35:33-34, NKJV).

The six "cities of refuge" were needed because society in that day had no police force to investigate crimes. It was the responsibility of each family to see to it that murders were avenged, but how could they tell whether it was a case of premeditated murder or accidental manslaughter? In the heat of anger a relative of the dead person might kill somebody who was really innocent of a capital crime.

Joshua set apart three cities of refuge on each side of the Jordan River. On the west side, Kedesh was farthest north, in the territory of Naphtali; Shechem was in the middle of the nation in the tribe of Manasseh; and Hebron was in the south in the tribe of Judah. On the east side of the Jordan, the cities were Golan in the north in Manasseh, Ramoth in Gad, and Bezer farther south in the tribe of Reuben. Since the Holy Land is about the size of the state of Maryland, you can see that nobody was very far from a city of refuge.

The law was really quite simple. Anybody who killed another person could flee to a city of refuge and be protected from "the avenger of blood" until the elders of the city could investigate the circumstances. If they found the fugitive guilty, he or she was put to death; but if they concluded that it was a case of manslaughter, the fugitive was allowed to live in the city and be protected from the avenger. Upon the death of the high priest, the fugitive could go home again. It was a case of forfeiting freedom in order to save his or her life.

Many students have seen in the cities of refuge a picture of our salvation in Jesus Christ, to whom we "have fled for refuge" (Heb. 6:18). The lost sinner, of course, is in danger of judgment because "the wages of sin is death" (Rom. 6:23). The avenger of blood is after him or her! God's appointed Savior is Jesus Christ (Acts 4:12), but the sinner must come to Him by faith in order to be saved (Matt. 11:28-30; John 6:37). The way to each city was kept open with roads that were cared for and marked (Deut. 19:3, NIV). God wanted it to be easy for the fugitives to find their way to safety.

Beyond this, the picture is one of *contrast*. When we come to Christ for salvation, there's no need for an investigation or a trial, because we *know* we're guilty; *and we admit it!* The only people Jesus can save are those who confess their guilt and throw themselves on His mercy.

If the fugitive prematurely left the city of refuge, he could be killed; but our salvation in Christ is not conditional. Our High Priest will *never* die, and we are forever secure. "But He, because He continues forever, has an unchangeable priesthood. Therefore He is also able to save to the uttermost those who come to God through Him, since He always lives to make intercession for them" (Heb. 7:24-25, NKJV).

The meanings of the names of the cities are interesting. Taking them in the order listed in Joshua 20:7-8, you have: Kedesh = "righteousness"; Shechem = "shoulder"; Hebron = "fellowship"; Bezer = "fortress" or "strong"; and Ramoth = "heights." Hebraists do not agree on what Golan means, but the *Gesenius Lexicon* says it means "exile."

These names then can be used to describe what sinners experience when they flee by faith to Jesus. First, He gives them His *righteousness,* and they can never be accused again. There is no condemnation! (Rom. 8:1) Like a shepherd, He carries them on His *shoulders,* and they enter into *fellowship* with Him. He is their *fortress,* and they are safe. They dwell in the *heights* even though they are *exiles,* pilgrims, and strangers in this world.

> **Lesson #7.** Unless you have fled by faith to Jesus Christ, you aren't saved! Since our sins put Jesus on the cross, all of us are guilty of His death. He is the only Savior, and apart from faith in Him, there is no salvation. Have you fled to Him?

Before leaving this theme, we should note that there is also an application to the nation of Israel. The nation was guilty of killing the Lord Jesus Christ, *but it was a sin of ignorance on the part of the people* (Acts 3:12-18). When Jesus prayed on the cross, "Father, forgive them; for they know not what they do" (Luke 23:34), He was declaring them guilty of manslaughter rather than murder (1 Cor. 2:7-8). The way was open for their forgiveness, and God gave the nation nearly forty years to repent before He brought judgment. This same principle applied to the Apostle Paul (1 Tim. 1:12-14). However, no lost sinner today can plead ignorance, because God has declared *the whole world* guilty and without excuse (Rom. 3:9-19).

4. The assignment of the levitical cities (Josh. 21:1-45)
As we noted before, the tribe of Levi didn't have territory assigned to it but was scattered throughout the land. This way, they could teach the people the Law and influence each of the tribes to be faithful to the Lord. But the Levites needed places to live and pastures for their cattle. Thus God assigned forty-eight cities for them to live in, along with a specific amount of land for pasture (Num. 35:1-5). The pasture land could not be sold, but their houses could be sold; and the Levites even had special privileges for redeeming their property (Lev. 23:32-34).

The two lists of levitical cities that we have—Joshua 21 and 1 Chronicles 6:54-81—do not always agree; but names of cities and spellings change over the years, and it's possible that from time to time new cities were selected and old ones abandoned.

There were forty-eight levitical cities, six of which were also cities of refuge. Each of the tribes contributed four cities, except Judah and Simeon, who together contributed nine, and Naphtali, who contributed three. The descendants of the three sons of Aaron—Kohath, Gershon and Marari—were assigned to the various cities, although other Jews also lived in them. In Numbers 26:62, the writer states that there were 23,000 Levites before Israel entered the land, a big crowd to distribute among forty-eight cities.

It was important that Israel have qualified and authorized people to minister in the tabernacle and later in the temple, and we must never minimize the teaching ministry of the priests and Levites (2 Chron. 17:7-9). Since the common people didn't own copies of the Scriptures, it was important that the Levites identify with the people and explain the Law to them. These levitical cities were so located that nobody was too far away from a man who could help them understand and apply the Law of Moses.

This long section in the Book of Joshua closes with three wonderful affirmations:

First, God was faithful and gave Israel the land (Josh. 20:43). He kept the covenant that He made, first with Abraham (Gen. 12:7) and then with his descendants.

Second, God gave Israel victory over all their enemies and then gave them the rest from war (Josh. 20:44; see 1:13, 15; 11:23). What the ten unbelieving spies at Kadesh Barnea said could never happen *did* happen, because Joshua and the people believed God and obeyed His Word.

Third, God kept His promises (20:45). At the close of his life Joshua would remind the people of this (23:14); and Solomon reminded them of it when he dedicated the temple (1 Kings 8:56).

As the people of God, we can claim these assurances by faith. God's covenant with us is not going to fail; God's power and wisdom can give us victory over every foe; and God's promises can be trusted, no matter what the circumstances may be.

The covenant of God, the power of God, the promises of God—these are the spiritual resources we can depend on as we claim our inheritance in Jesus Christ.

ELEVEN

And When the Battle's Over

I remember VE-Day, May 8, 1945, when we heard President Truman announce over the radio: "General Eisenhower informs me that the forces of Germany have surrendered to the United Nations. The flags of freedom fly all over Europe."

I remember VJ-Day, August 14, 1945, when the downtown area of our city was jammed with people and total strangers were hugging one another and cheering. The Japanese had agreed to the Allied terms of surrender, and the war was over. My two brothers serving in the Marine Corps would be coming home!

The soldiers from the tribes of Reuben, Gad, and the half tribe of Manasseh must have been especially euphoric when the Jewish conquest of Canaan ended. For over seven years they had been away from their families on the other side of the Jordan, and now the victorious soldiers were free to go home.

But their return home was not without incident. In fact, what they did, well-meaning as it was, almost provoked another war. Let's consider the events involved and the lessons we can learn from them.

1. Their honorable discharge (Josh. 22:1-8)

"In defeat unbeatable; in victory unbearable." That's the way Sir Winston Churchill described a British army officer famous in the Second World War. The first half of the description would apply to Joshua, because he knew how to win victory out of defeat. But the last half doesn't apply at all; for as commander of the Lord's army, Joshua was magnanimous in the way he treated his troops after the victory. An Italian proverb says, "It's the blood of the soldier that makes the general great." But this general made his soldiers great! This is clearly seen in the way he discharged the tribes who lived on the east side of the Jordan.

He commended them (Josh. 22:1-3). These two and a half tribes had promised Moses that they would remain in the army until all the land was conquered, and they kept their promise (Num. 32; Deut. 3:12-20). After the death of Moses, they pledged that same loyalty to Joshua, their new leader (Josh. 1:12-18). These tribes had been loyal to Moses, to Joshua, and to their brothers from the other tribes. "For a long time now—to this very day—you have not deserted your brothers but have carried out the mission the Lord your God gave you" (22:3, NIV).

Why had they been so loyal to their leaders and fellow soldiers? Because they were first of all loyal to the Lord their God. It was *His* mission they were carrying out and *His* name they were seeking to glorify. In the service of the Lord, far above our devotion to a leader, a cause, or even a nation is our devotion to the Lord. "And whatever you do, do it heartily, as to the Lord and not to men, knowing that from the Lord you will receive the reward of the inheritance; for you serve the Lord Christ" (Col. 3:23-24, NKJV).

He discharged them (Josh. 22:4). Having fulfilled their mission and kept their promise, the tribes were now free to go home; for God had given His people rest. The concept of *rest* is important in the Book of Joshua and means much more than simply the end of the war. The word carries with it the meaning of both *victory* and *security,* and it involved Israel having their "resting place" in the land. God promised to give His people rest (Ex. 33:14; Deut. 12:9-10; 25:19; Josh. 1:13, 15), and He kept His promise (11:23; 14:15; 21:44; 22:4; 23:1).

The spiritual application of this *rest* for God's people today is made in Hebrews 3 and 4. When we trust Christ as Savior, we enter into *rest* because we're no longer at war with God (Rom. 5:1). When we yield ourselves completely to Him and claim our inheritance by faith, we enter into a deeper *rest* and enjoy our spiritual riches in Christ. (See Matt. 11:28-32 for our Lord's invitation.) When we *come to Him,* He gives us rest. When we *take His yoke of discipleship,* we find that deeper rest.

Imagine what it would be like for these soldiers to return home after being away for so many years! Think of the love they would experience, the joys they would find, the treasures they would share! That's just a small picture of what happens when the children of God enter into the rest God gives to those who will yield their all to Him and trust His Word.

He admonished them (Josh. 22:5). Like any good leader, Joshua was more concerned about the spiritual walk of his people than anything else. The army had experienced victory in Canaan because Joshua loved the Lord and obeyed His Word (1:7-8), and that would be the "open secret" of Israel's continued peace and prosperity. Just as they had been diligent in battle, obeying their commander, so they must be diligent in worship, obeying the Lord their God. This was the promise each of the tribes made to the Lord at Mt. Gerizim and Mt. Ebal.

The motive for their obedience had to be love for the Lord

their God. If they loved Him, then they would delight in walking in all His ways and obeying all His commandments. Instead of trying to serve two masters, they would cling (cleave) to the Lord and serve Him alone, with all their heart and soul. Jesus said this was the first and greatest commandment (Matt. 22:36-38); therefore, to disobey it would mean to commit the greatest sin. "If you love Me, keep My commandments" (John 14:15, NKJV).

He blessed them (Josh. 22:6-8). It was the ministry of the high priest to bless God's people (Num. 6:22-27), but the common people could invoke God's blessing on others, especially a leader upon his people or a father upon his family (Gen. 27:4; 48:9; 2 Sam. 6:18, 20; 1 Kings 8:55). What a sight to see a great general asking God's blessing on his troops!

But this blessing also involved sharing the rich spoils of battle with them and their family members back home. It was the custom in Israel that those who stayed home, or who couldn't participate in the battle for some good reason, also shared the spoils (Num. 31:25-27; 1 Sam. 30:23-25). After all, these people had protected the home cities and kept the machinery of the community going while the men had been out fighting, and it was only fair that they share in the spoils.

Indeed, for the two and a half tribes that lived east of the Jordan, it was an honorable discharge.

2. Their honest concern (Josh. 22:9-10)

As the men of Reuben, Gad, and the half tribe of Manasseh made their way east and passed landmarks that brought back memories of the great things God had done, their hearts began to disturb them. Happy as they were to be going home, it wasn't easy to say good-bye to their brothers and leave behind the nearness of the priesthood and the tabernacle. They were leaving the land that God had promised to bless. Yes, they were going home to the land that they had chosen for themselves; but somehow they began to feel isolated from the nation of Israel.

When you read and ponder Numbers 32, you discover that there is no record that Moses consulted the Lord about this decision. The thing Moses was most concerned about was that the men of Reuben, Gad, and Manasseh do their share in fighting the enemy and conquering the Promised Land; and this they agreed to do. Moses' first response was that of anger mingled with fear, lest God judge the nation as He had at Kadesh Barnea. Perhaps this first reaction was the right one.

There's no question that Canaan was God's appointed land for His people; anything short of Canaan wasn't what He wanted for them. The two and a half tribes made their decision, not on the basis of spiritual values, but on the basis of material gain; for the land east of the Jordan was ideal for raising cattle. I'm reminded of the decision Lot made when he pitched his tent toward Sodom (Gen. 13:10-11). In both instances, the people walked by sight and not by faith.

By making this decision, the people of Reuben, Gad, and Manasseh divided the nation and separated themselves from the blessings of the land of Canaan. They were farther away from the tabernacle and closer to the enemy. They became what I call "borderline believers." You'll recall that Egypt represents the world and Canaan the believer's inheritance in Christ. The wilderness wanderings represent the experience of believers who don't enter by faith into the *rest* God has for them (Heb. 3–4). The two and a half tribes portray believers who have experienced the blessings and battles of Canaan—their inheritance in Christ—but prefer to live on the border, outside God's appointed place of blessing.

"Faith can never be satisfied with anything short of the true position and portion of God's people," wrote C.H. MacIntosh in his *Notes on Numbers.* "An undecided, half-and-half

Christian is more inconsistent than an open, out-and-out worldling or infidel" (pp. 457, 460).

How did they decide to solve the problem which they themselves had created? By building a large altar of stones by the Jordan River, on the Canaan side, as a reminder to everybody that the two and a half tribes also belonged to the nation of Israel. Had these tribes been living in the land of Canaan where they belonged, nobody would have questioned their nationality. But living outside the land, they gave the impression that they were not Israelites.

This is now the eighth memorial erected in Canaan (Josh. 4:9, 20-24; 7:26; 8:29-32 [three memorials]; 10:27). But it's unfortunate when believers have to resort to artificial means to let people know they're God's people. In recent years we've seen a spate of "religious" bumper stickers, jewelry, decals, and other items (including mirrors and combs with Bible verses on them), all of which are supposed to help identify the owners with Jesus Christ. While these things might occasionally open doors of opportunity for witness, how much better it would be if our Spirit-led conduct and speech made the lost sit up and take notice. When we're living as God wants us to live, we're salt and light; and the Lord uses our witness for His glory.

If the people of Reuben, Gad, and Manasseh faithfully attended the feasts in Jerusalem (Ex. 23:17), honored the Lord by obeying His Word, and talked about His Word in their homes (Deut. 6:6-9), they would be able to raise their children to know and serve the Lord. The altar on the Jordan bank, however, was no guarantee of such success.

3. Their humble submission (Josh. 22:11-29)
The alarm (Josh. 22:11-14). The word traveled quickly that the tribes east of the Jordan had erected an altar. While these Transjordanic tribes had been very sincere in what they did,

their action was misunderstood; and the other tribes prepared for possible war. But wisely, they waited while an official delegation investigated what was going on. "He who answers a matter before he hears it, it is folly and shame to him" (Prov. 18:13, NKJV).

The delegation of ten princes, one from each tribe, was led by Phinehas, the son of the high priest, a man who had already proved himself courageous in defending the Law of the Lord (Num. 25; Ps. 106:30-31). It was the responsibility of the tribal leaders and the priests to investigate every situation in Israel that appeared to be a breach of the Law (Deut. 13). God had instructed the Jews to destroy the altars of the heathen nations in Canaan and not to build altars of their own. There was to be one altar of sacrifice at the one sanctuary that God had appointed (Deut. 12; Lev. 17:8-9).

The appeal (Josh. 22:15-20). It's likely that Phinehas made the speech, but note that his address represented the agreement of all the tribes. Phinehas called what they had done a *trespass* (vv. 16, 20, 22 [*transgression,* KJV], 31), which means "an act of treachery." Joshua had commended these two and a half tribes for their loyalty, and now they had proved faithless. They had *turned away* (vv. 16, 18, 23, 29), which meant they were no longer following the Lord (see v. 5). This word carries the idea of "backsliding," gradually moving away from the Lord.

The strongest word used was *rebel* (vv. 16, 18-19 [twice], 22, 29), which means deliberately resisting God's will and disobeying His Law. In building an unauthorized altar, these two and a half tribes were guilty of apostasy. "For rebellion is as the sin of witchcraft, and stubbornness is as iniquity and idolatry" (1 Sam. 15:23).

From the nation's recent history Phinehas cited two serious cases of rebellion as warning to these tribes. The first was the participation of Israel in the heathen rites of the

Moabites, when the men committed harlotry with the Moabite women (Josh. 22:17; Num. 25). As a result, 24,000 people died. The second was the sin of Achan after the victory at Jericho, when he deliberately took the spoils that belonged to the Lord (Josh. 22:20; see Josh. 7). His sin led to defeat at Ai and the deaths of thirty-six Jewish soldiers. It also led to his own death and that of the members of his family.

The delegation gave a wise word of counsel: "Come over and dwell with us, because we have the Lord's tabernacle in our land" (22:19, paraphrase). No man-made altar could substitute for the presence of the Lord among His people in His tabernacle. It's too bad the two and a half tribes didn't take this advice and claim their inheritance within the land that God had promised to bless (Deut. 11:10-32).

The argument (Josh. 22:21-29). The accused tribes invoked the name of the Lord six times as they replied to the charges; and in so doing, they used the three fundamental names for the Lord: "El [the Mighty One], Elohim [God], Jehovah [the Lord]." It was a solemn oath that their intentions were pure and that the Lord knew their hearts.

Of course, the fact that the Lord knows our hearts, and that we've taken an oath, is no guarantee that our actions are right, *because we don't know our own hearts* (Jer. 17:9). All sorts of questionable activities can be shielded by, "But the Lord knows my heart!" Paul gives us the right approach in 2 Corinthians 8:21; "For we are taking pains to do what is right, not only in the eyes of the Lord but also in the eyes of men" (NIV). When a whole nation misinterprets what is supposed to be a good deed, and it brings them to the brink of war, then there must be something wrong with that deed.

The accused tribes made it clear that they weren't setting up a rival religion because the altar they built wasn't for sacrifices. Rather, they were putting up a witness that would remind the tribes west of the Jordan that Reuben, Gad, and

Manasseh were a part of the Jewish nation.

It's interesting that the Transjordanic tribes pointed to the children as their concern. But it wasn't *their* children who would ask, "What have we to do with the Lord God of Israel?" No, their children would be provoked by the children of the tribes in Canaan! Reuben, Gad, and Manasseh were not even living in the land of God's choice, *yet they feared lest the children across the river would lead their children astray!* It seems to me that the danger was just the opposite.

Not only did the Transjordanic tribes accuse their fellow Jews of having worldly children, but they even accused God of creating the problem in the first place! "For the Lord has made the Jordan a border between you and us" (Josh. 22:25, NKJV). No! *They were the ones who had made the Jordan River the dividing line!* In choosing to live east of the Jordan, the two and a half tribes separated themselves from their own people and from the land God had given to all of them. They put their cattle ahead of their children and their fellow Jews, but they blamed God and the other tribes for the problem that they created.

But what kind of "witness" was this huge pile of stones? Was it a witness to the unity of the nation and to the obedience of the Transjordanic tribes? No, it was a witness to *expediency,* the wisdom of man in trying to enjoy "the best of both worlds." The two and a half tribes talked piously about their children, but it was their wealth that really motivated their decision to live east of the Jordan.

Somewhere near this "witness altar" were the twelve stones that the men had carried from the midst of the Jordan River (4:20-24). It reminded the Jews that they had crossed the river and buried their past forever. Reuben, Gad, and the half tribe of Manasseh had crossed the river *and gone back again.* Their "altar" contradicted the altar that Joshua had erected to the glory of God. "If then you were raised with

Christ, seek those things which are above, where Christ is, sitting at the right hand of God" (Col. 3:1, NKJV).

4. Their happy agreement (Josh. 22:30-34)

Phinehas was pleased, the delegation was pleased, and the Children of Israel across the Jordan were pleased; *but was the Lord pleased?* The delegation rejoiced that the purpose of the altar was for witness and not sacrifice, and this seemed to settle the matter. They rejoiced that God wouldn't send judgment to the land (v. 31) and that there would be no civil war in Israel (v. 33). *But the nation was divided, in spite of the "altar of witness."* Like Abraham and Lot (Gen. 13), part of the nation had a spiritual outlook while the other part was concerned with material things.

"Peace at any price" isn't God's will for His people. This decision in Gilead was made on the basis of human wisdom and not God's truth. "But the wisdom that is from above is *first pure,* then peaceable" (James 3:17, italics mine). *The peace that God's people achieve at the price of purity and truth is only a dangerous truce that eventually explodes into painful division.* There is always a place in human relations for loving conciliation, but never for cowardly compromise. "I charge you before God and the Lord Jesus Christ and the elect angels that you observe these things without prejudice, doing nothing with partiality" (1 Tim. 5:21, NKJV).

The Transjordanic tribes named their altar "A witness between us that the Lord is God" (NIV). (The Hebrew word *edh* means "witness.") But if the Lord is God, why didn't they obey Him and live in the land He had appointed for them? The stones may have been a witness, but the people certainly were not. Surrounded by heathen nations and separated from their brothers and sisters across the river, these tribes quickly fell into idolatry and were eventually taken by Assyria (1 Chron. 5:25-26).

On September 30, 1938, British Prime Minister Sir Neville Chamberlain, just back from Germany, told a gathering at 10 Downing Street: "My good friends, this is the second time in our history that there has come back from Germany to Downing Street peace with honor. I believe it is peace for our time. We thank you from the bottom of our hearts. And now I recommend you to go home and sleep quietly in your beds."

Less than a year later, England was at war with Germany; and World War II had burst upon the world.

Church history is replete with agreements and accords that magnified unity over purity and truth, and therefore never lasted. Whether in our personal relationships in our homes and churches, or in our nation, the only peace that lasts is peace that is based on truth and purity. It's a peace that demands sacrifice and courage, and a willingness to stand up for God's Word; but the results are worth it.

The well-known Bible commentator, Matthew Henry, said it best: "Peace is such a precious jewel that I would give anything for it but truth."

The Way of All the Earth

The well-known psychoanalyst Eric Fromm wrote in *Man for Himself*, "To die is poignantly bitter, but the idea of having to die without having lived is unbearable."

Joshua the son of Nun had lived! His long life started in Egyptian bondage and ended in a worship service in the Promised Land. In between those events God had used him to lead Israel in defeating the enemy, conquering the land, and claiming the promised inheritance. With the Apostle Paul, Joshua could sincerely say, "I have fought a good fight, I have finished my course, I have kept the faith" (2 Tim. 4:7, KJV).

Joshua was about to go "the way of all the earth" (Josh. 23:14), the way you and I must go if the Lord doesn't return first. But at the end of a long and full life, Joshua's greatest concern wasn't himself. His greatest concern was his people and their relationship to the Lord. He didn't want to leave until he had challenged them once again to love the Lord and keep His commandments. His life's work would be in vain if they failed to keep the covenant and enjoy the blessings of the Promised Land.

He first called a meeting of the leaders of the nation (v. 2), either at Shiloh or at his home in Ephraim, and warned them what would happen if they deserted the Lord. Then he gathered "all the tribes of Israel to Shechem" (24:1) and gave a farewell address which reviewed the history of Israel, starting with Abraham, and challenged the people to love the Lord and serve Him alone. In these two addresses Joshua emphasized three important topics.

1. Israel's future dangers (Josh. 23:1-16)

Having assembled the leaders of the nation, Joshua presented them with two scenarios: Obey the Lord, and He will bless you and keep you in the land; disobey Him, and He will judge you and remove you from the land. These were the terms of the covenant God had made with Israel at Mt. Sinai, which Moses had repeated on the Plains of Moab, and which Israel had reaffirmed at Mt. Ebal and Mt. Gerizim.

Joshua's emphasis was on possessing the land (v. 5) and enjoying its blessings (vv. 13, 15-16). While Israel had gained control of Canaan, there still remained territory to possess and pockets of resistance to overcome. (See 13:1-13; 15:63; 16:10; 17:12-13; 18:3; Jud. 1–2.) The task of the tribes wasn't finished! The great danger, of course, was that the people of Israel would gradually change their attitudes toward the pagan nations around them and start accepting their ways and imitating them.

To counteract this danger, Joshua gave the people three strong motives for remaining a separated people and serving the Lord faithfully.

What the Lord did for Israel (Josh. 23:3-4). From the day that Israel left Egypt, the Lord had fought for His people and delivered them from their enemies. He drowned the Egyptian army in the sea and then defeated the Amalekites who attacked the Jews soon after they left Egypt (Ex. 17). The Lord defeated all of Israel's enemies as the nation marched toward

Canaan, and He gave His people victory over the nations in the Promised Land.

This review of history reminded Israel of two great facts: Those Gentile nations were God's enemies and therefore must be Israel's enemies; and the same God who overcame the enemy in the past could help Israel overcome them in the future. God had never failed His people; and, if they would trust Him and obey His Word, He would help them completely conquer the land. "For the Lord your God is He who has fought for you" (Josh. 23:3, NKJV).

This is a good reminder to God's people today. As we read the Bible and see what God did in the past for those who trusted Him, it encourages us to trust Him today and face all our enemies with courage and confidence. The Presbyterian missionary leader A.T. Pierson used to say that "history is His story"; and this is true. From age to age, God may change His methods; but His character never changes, and He can be trusted.

What the Lord said to Israel (Josh. 23:5-10). The secret of Joshua's success, and therefore the reason for Israel's victories, was his devotion to the Word of God (vv. 6, 14; see 1:7-9, 13-18; 8:30-35; 11:12, 15; 24:26-27). He obeyed God's commandments and believed God's promises, and God worked on his behalf. But even more, his devotion to the Word of God enabled Joshua to get to know God better, to love Him, and to want to please Him. It isn't enough to know the Word of God. We must also know the God of the Word and grow in our fellowship with Him.

God kept all His promises, and He had every right to expect Israel to keep all His commandments as well. Some of God's promises are unconditional, but some of them are conditional and depend on our obedience for their fulfillment. Israel entered and conquered the land as the fulfillment of God's promise, but their enjoyment of the land depended on their obedience to the Law of the Lord. God would enable them to claim all their inheritance if they would obey Him with all their hearts.

The most important thing was that Israel remain a separated people and not be infected by the wickedness of the Gentile nations around them (23:7-8; see Ex. 34:10-17; Deut. 7:2-4). Joshua warned them that their disobedience would be a gradual thing. First they would associate with these nations in a familiar way; then they would start discussing their religious practices; and before long Israel would be worshiping the false gods of the enemy. The Jewish men would then start marrying women from these pagan nations, and the line of separation between God's people and the world would be completely erased. Imagine the folly of *worshiping the gods of the defeated enemy!*

All of us feel the pressures of the world around us, trying to force us to conform (Rom. 12:1-21; 1 John 2:15-17); and it takes courage to defy the crowd and stay true to the Lord (Josh. 23:7). But it also takes love for the Lord and a desire to please Him (v. 8). The word translated "cleave" in verse 8 is used in Genesis 2:24 to describe a husband's relationship to his wife. Israel was "married" to Jehovah at Mt. Sinai (Jer. 2:1-3; Ezek. 16) and was expected to be a faithful spouse and cleave to the Lord (Deut. 4:4; 10:20; 11:22; 13:4). How tragic that she became an unfaithful wife, a prostitute, as she turned to the gods of other nations.

The promise in Joshua 23:10 is quoted from Deuteronomy 32:30, which shows how well Joshua knew the Word of God. (See also Lev. 26:7-8.) He meditated on God's Word day and night (Josh. 1:8; Ps. 1:2) and hid it in his heart (Ps. 119:11).

What the Lord would do to Israel (Josh. 23:11-16). The Word of God is like a two-edged sword (Heb. 4:12): If we obey it, God will bless and help us; if we disobey it, God will chasten us until we submit to Him. If we love the Lord (Josh. 23:11), we'll want to obey Him and please Him; so the essential thing is that we cultivate a satisfying relationship with God.

Joshua reminded the people that God's Word never fails, whether it's the Word of promise for blessing or the Word of promise for chastening. Both are evidences of His love, for "whom the Lord loveth He chasteneth" (Prov. 3:11-12; Heb. 12:6). Charles Spurgeon said, "God will not allow His children to sin successfully."

Moses had warned Israel against compromising with the evil nations in the land (Ex. 23:20-33; 34:10-17; Deut. 7:12-26), and Joshua reaffirmed that warning (Josh. 23:13). If Israel began to mingle with these nations, two things would happen: God would remove His blessing, and Israel would be defeated; and these nations would bring distress and defeat to Israel. Joshua used vivid words like *snares, traps, scourges,* and *thorns* to impress the Jews with the suffering they would experience if they disobeyed the Lord. The final stroke of chastening would be Israel's removal from their land to a land of exile. After all, if you want to live and worship like the Gentiles, then live with the Gentiles! This happened when God permitted Babylon to conquer Judah, destroy Jerusalem, and take thousands of the Jews into exile in Babylon.

Three times in this brief address Joshua called Canaan "this good land" (vv. 13, 15-16). When God called Moses at the burning bush, He promised to take Israel into a "good land" (Ex. 3:8); and Joshua and Caleb described Canaan as "a good land" after forty days of investigation (Num. 14:7). In his farewell message Moses used the phrase "good land" at least ten times (Deut. 1:25, 35; 3:25; 4:21-22; 6:18; 8:7, 10; 9:6; 11:17). The argument is obvious: Since God has given us such a good land, the least we can do is live to please Him.

Meditating on the goodness of God is a strong motivation for obedience. James connects the goodness of God with our resisting of temptation (James 1:13-17), and Nathan took the same approach when he confronted King David with his sins (2 Sam. 12:1-15). It was not his own badness but his father's goodness that brought the prodigal son to repentance and then back home (Luke 15:17). "The goodness of God leads you to repentance" (Rom. 2:4, NKJV). The danger is that the material blessings from the Lord can so possess our hearts that we focus on the gifts and forget the Giver, and this leads to sin (Deut. 8).

Joshua's three main admonitions in this address need to be heeded by God's people today: Keep God's Word (Josh. 23:6), cleave to the Lord (v. 8), and love the Lord (v. 11). Too many Christians have not only compromised with the enemy but also have capitulated to the enemy, and the Lord is not first in their lives.

2. Israel's past blessings (Josh. 24:1-13)

In the April 15, 1978 issue of *Saturday Review,* the late author and editor Norman Cousins called history "a vast early warning system"; and philosopher George Santayana said, "Those who cannot remember the past are condemned to repeat it." A knowledge of their roots is very important to the Jews because they are God's chosen people with a destiny to fulfill in this world.

Shechem was the ideal location for this moving farewell address by Israel's great leader. It was at Shechem that God promised Abraham that his descendants would inherit the land (Gen. 12:6-7), and there Jacob built an altar (33:20). Shechem was located between Mt. Ebal and Mt. Gerizim, where the people of Israel had reaffirmed their commitment to the Lord (Josh. 8:30-35). Shechem was indeed "holy ground" to the Israelites.

If *nation* and *land* were the key words in Joshua's first address, then *the Lord* is the major focus in this second address; for Joshua refers to the Lord twenty-one times. In fact, in 24:2-13, it is the Lord who speaks as Joshua reviews the history of the nation. Another key word is *serve,* used fifteen times in this address. Jehovah gave them their land and would bless them in their land if they loved Him and served Him.

God chose Israel (Josh. 24:1-4). Abraham and his family were idolaters when God called Abraham to leave Ur of the Chaldees and go to Canaan (Gen. 11:27–12:9). "The God of glory appeared unto our father Abraham," declared Stephen in his own farewell speech (Acts 7:2), reminding the Jews that their national identity was *an act of God's grace.* Abraham didn't seek after God and discover Him; it was God who came to Abraham! There was nothing special about the Jews that God should choose them (Deut. 7:1-11; 26:1-11; 32:10); and this fact should have kept them humble and obedient.

"You did not choose Me," Jesus told His disciples, "but I chose you and appointed you" (John 15:16, NKJV). Believers were chosen in Christ "before the foundation of the world" (Eph. 1:4) and are called "God's elect" (Rom. 8:33; Titus 1:1). One of my professors in seminary used to say, "Try to explain election and you may lose your mind, but explain it away and you may lose your soul." No matter what "school" of theology we belong to, all of us must admit that *God takes the first step in our salvation.*

Abraham's firstborn son was Ishmael (Gen. 16), but God rejected him and gave His covenant to Isaac, the child of Abraham and Sarah's old age (17–18, 21). Isaac had two sons, Jacob and Esau; and God chose Jacob. Paul called these choices God's purpose "according to election" (Rom. 9:11). Esau became the ancestor of the Edomites in Mount Seir, and Jacob became the father of the twelve tribes of Israel. Eventually, the Children of Israel went to Egypt, where God made them into a great nation.

One of the repeated titles for God in the Book of Joshua is

"the Lord God of Israel," used fifteen times (7:13, 19-20; 8:30; 9:18-19; 10:40, 42; 13:14, 33; 14:14; 22:16, 24; 24:2, 23). The Jews were indeed an elect and a special people; for the Lord of heaven chose to associate His great name with them and be their God.

God delivered Israel (Josh. 24:5-7). God sent Joseph ahead to Egypt to preserve the nation during the famine (Ps. 105:16-22), and then He sent Moses and Aaron to deliver the nation from bondage (vv. 23-45). Egypt had been saved from starvation because of the Jews; but instead of being grateful, the rulers of Egypt eventually enslaved the Jews and made their lives bitter (Ex. 3:7-9). All of this was a fulfillment of what God had promised to Abraham centuries before (Gen. 15:1-17), but their suffering in Egypt only made the Israelites multiply more.

God judged the gods and rulers of Egypt by sending ten plagues to the land, climaxing with the death of the firstborn (Ex. 7–12). Only then did stubborn Pharaoh give the Jews permission to leave the land, but then he changed his mind and sent his army after them. God not only brought His people *out,* but He also led them *through* the Red Sea and drowned the Egyptian army in its waters (chaps. 14–15).

God instructed His people to observe the Passover as an annual reminder of their redemption from Egyptian bondage (chaps. 12–13). In his farewell speech Moses frequently reminded the Jews that they had once been slaves in Egypt but the Lord had set them free (5:15; 6:12; 8:14; 13:5, 10; 15:15; 16:3, 6; 20:1; 24:22). It does a believer good to remember what it was like to be in bondage to sin and then to rejoice in the redemption that was purchased so dearly for us on the cross. It's a dangerous thing to take the gift of salvation for granted.

God guided Israel (Josh. 24:8-10). God brought Israel out that He might bring them in (Deut. 6:23). His goal for them was the Promised Land, but their sin at Kadesh Barnea caused them to wander in the wilderness until the old unbelieving generation had died off. As Israel marched behind the ark of God, the Lord defeated their enemies. When Balaam tried to curse Israel, God turned the curse into a blessing (Num. 22–24; Deut. 23:5; Neh. 13:2). Whether Satan came against Israel as the lion (the army of the Amorites) or as the serpent (the curses of Balaam), the Lord defeated him.

God gave them their land (Josh. 24:11-13). The same God who took Israel through the Red Sea also took them across the Jordan River and into their inheritance. Except for a temporary defeat at Ai (Josh. 7), and a humiliating compromise with Gibeon (chap. 9), Joshua and his army defeated every enemy in the land because the Lord was with them.

The "hornet" mentioned in 24:12 (see Ex. 23:28; Deut. 7:20) may have been the insect whose sting is extremely painful, but it's possible that the word is an image of something else. Invading armies are compared to bees (Deut. 1:44; Ps. 118:12; Isa. 7:18), and some students think that's the meaning here. God sent other armies into Canaan to weaken the people and prepare them for the invasion of Israel.

But perhaps the hornets better represent the reports that came to Canaan of Israel's conquests, reports that frightened and almost paralyzed the inhabitants of the land. The words of Rahab describe the panic of the Canaanites because of what they heard about Israel: "And as soon as we had heard these things, our hearts did melt, neither did there remain any more courage in any man, because of you" (Josh. 2:11; see 5:1 and 9:24). God had promised to do this and He kept His promise (Deut. 2:25).

In Joshua 24:13, God's words remind us of what Moses said to Israel in Deuteronomy 6:10ff. Once again, the emphasis is on the goodness of God and all that He did for Israel because He loved them. When the Jews started taking their blessings for granted, they began drifting away from sincere worship of the Lord. A grateful heart is a strong defense against the devil's temptations.

3. Israel's present responsibilities (Josh. 24:14-33)

One of the key words in this section is *serve*, used fifteen times. To serve God means to fear Him, obey Him, and worship only Him. It means to love Him and fix your heart upon Him, obeying Him because you want to and not because you have to.

Decision (Josh. 24:14-18). Joshua made it clear that the people of Israel had to make a decision to serve the Lord God of Israel. There could be no neutrality. But if they served the Lord, then they would have to get rid of the false gods that some of them secretly were worshiping. Even after the great experience of the Exodus, some of the Jews still sacrificed to the gods of Egypt (Lev. 17:7; Amos 5:25-26; Acts 7:42-43; Ezek. 20:6-8). Jacob had given this same warning to his family (Gen. 35:2), and Samuel would give the same admonition in his day (1 Sam. 7:3ff).

Joshua wasn't suggesting that the people could choose to worship the false gods of the land, and God would accept it; for there was no other option but to serve Jehovah. Being a wise and spiritual man, Joshua knew that everybody must worship something or someone, whether they realized it or not, because humanity is "incurably religious." If the Jews didn't worship the true God, they would end up worshiping the false gods of the wicked nations in Canaan. His point was that *they couldn't do both.*

The people assured Joshua that they wanted to worship and serve only the Lord God of Israel, and they gave their reasons. The Lord had delivered them from Egypt, brought them through the wilderness, and taken them into their Promised Land. (The first half of Joshua's address [Josh.

24:1-13] had made an impression on them!) Joshua had declared that he and his house would serve only the Lord (v. 15), and the people said, "Therefore will we also serve the Lord; for he is our God" (v. 18).

Devotion (Josh. 24:19-28). When the former generation had met the Lord at Mt. Sinai, they had said, "All that the Lord has spoken we will do" (Ex. 19:8, NKJV). But a few weeks later, they were worshiping a golden calf! Joshua knew that it was easy for the people to *promise* obedience to the Lord, but it was quite something else for them to actually *do* it. His stern words were meant to curb their overconfidence and make them look honestly into their own hearts (Josh. 24:19).

Israel was "married" to Jehovah, and He would not tolerate any rivals in their hearts. He is a jealous God (Ex. 20:5) and a holy God, and He could never permit them to be divided in their loyalty. Just as a husband and wife are faithful to their marriage vows and jealously guard their mate's affection, so Israel and the Lord had to be faithful to each other.

Joshua warned them what would happen if they didn't get rid of their idols: They would eventually forsake the Lord, and then He would have to chasten them. They would lose all the blessings He had so graciously given them in the Promised Land. Their great need was to cleanse their hearts of allegiance to other gods and to incline their hearts only to the Lord (Josh. 24:23). If they persisted in their hidden disloyalty, God would not forgive them (Ex. 23:21) but would punish them for their sins.

Three times the people affirmed their desire to serve only the Lord (Josh. 24:16-18, 21, 24), and Joshua took them at their word. So that they wouldn't forget this solemn covenant with Jehovah, Joshua wrote it in the Book of the Law and then set up a large stone as a perpetual witness to their agreement. This is the ninth and last memorial mentioned in the Book of Joshua. The nine memorials are:

1. The stones in the midst of the Jordan (4:9).
2. The stones on the western bank of the Jordan (4:20-24).
3. The stones in the Valley of Achor (7:26).
4. The heap of stones at Ai (8:29).
5. The altar on Mt. Ebal (8:30).
6. The stones of the law on Mt. Ebal (8:32).
7. The stones at the cave at Makkedah (10:27).
8. The altar built by the Transjordanic tribes (22:10ff).
9. Joshua's stone of witness (24:26-28).

There's certainly nothing unbiblical about God's people memorializing a wonderful event or a sacred decision, so long as the memorial doesn't become the focus of idolatrous worship. It's good to remember what the Lord did and how we responded, but we must never live in the past. Religious traditions can be helpful or hurtful, depending on how we use them.

The book closes with three burials. Joshua died at the age of 110 and was buried in his own inheritance. Eleazar the high priest (Num. 20:28) died and was also buried in Ephraim, near Shiloh, where his son Phinehas had property. The bones of Joseph were buried in Shechem in the plot of ground Jacob had bought from Hamor (Gen. 33:19). Shechem became an important city for Ephraim and Manasseh, who were the two sons of Joseph. Thus it was fitting that their great ancestor be buried there. (See Gen. 50:25; Ex. 13:19; Heb. 11:22.)

Moses had named Joshua as his successor, but it's significant that God didn't tell Joshua to appoint a successor. The elders who had served with Joshua guided the nation after his death, but then the people went astray and began to disobey the Lord and worship the false gods of the Canaanites (Jud. 2:6-15). Why didn't the next generation know the Lord and what He had done for Israel? *Because the people of Joshua's generation failed to keep their promise and teach their children and grandchildren to fear and serve the Lord.*

God kept His promise and chastened His people, first by bringing other nations into the land (vv. 14-19), and then by taking the Jews out of their land, the Northern Kingdom to Assyria and the Southern Kingdom to Babylon. But one day the Lord will regather His people Israel and establish them in their land (Isa. 11–12; 51–52; Ezek. 36:24ff). Then "the earth shall be filled with the knowledge of the glory of the Lord, as the waters cover the sea" (Hab. 2:14).

A Great Life in Review

In his *Autobiography,* Mark Twain wrote: "Biographies are but the clothes and buttons of the man—the biography of the man himself cannot be written."

The Book of Joshua is not a biography of Joshua in the strictest sense, but it certainly tells us a great deal about this godly man. Like the rest of the Old Testament Scriptures, this book was written both to warn us (1 Cor. 10:11) and to encourage us (Rom. 15:4). Therefore, we ought to take time to review Joshua's life and ministry and learn from him lessons that will help us know the Lord better and serve Him more effectively.

1. Joshua's preparation

When God wants to accomplish something, He prepares a servant for the task and prepares the task for His servant. The Lord invested seventeen years preparing Joseph for His work in Egypt and eighty years getting Moses ready for forty years of ministry to the people of Israel. David experienced many years of trials and testings before he ascended the throne of Israel. "A prepared servant for a prepared place" is God's approach to ministry.

What were some of the "tools" God used to prepare Joshua for his ministry?

Suffering. Joshua was born into Egyptian slavery and knew what it was to suffer. In Exodus 3:7-9, the Lord's words make it clear that the Jews experienced great affliction in Egypt and cried out to God for deliverance. Nevertheless they had at least three encouragements as they suffered: God's promise to Abraham that his descendants would inherit the land (Gen. 12:7); God's prophecy concerning their deliverance from bondage (15:12-17; see Deut. 4:20); and Joseph's words concerning Israel's deliverance and possession of the Promised Land (Gen. 50:22-26).

God's pattern for life is that suffering must come before glory. This was true of our Savior (Luke 24:26; 1 Peter 1:11) and it is true of His people (1 Peter 4:13; 5:10). When we suffer in the will of God and depend on His grace, that suffering has a maturing and purifying effect on our lives. Sadly, we have too many leaders today who proudly display their medals, but they can't show you any scars. Our Lord's Calvary wounds are now glorified in heaven, eternal reminders that suffering and glory go together in the purposes of God.

Of itself, suffering doesn't make people better. Sometimes it makes them bitter. But when suffering is mixed with faith and God's grace, then it becomes a wonderful tool for building godly character (2 Cor. 12:1-10). If suffering alone gave people wisdom and character, then our world would be a far better place, because everybody suffers in one way or another. When we accept our suffering as a gift from God and use it for His glory, then it can work in us and for us to accomplish the will of God.

Submission. Joshua knew how to submit to authority. As leader of the Jewish army, he followed Moses' orders and defeated the Amalekites (Ex. 17:8-16). As Moses' "assistant" for many years (24:13), Joshua stayed with his master and served him faithfully. God's pattern for leadership is summarized in Matthew 25:21, and that pattern still stands today: when we prove ourselves faithful as servants over a few things, then God can make us rulers over many things. Joshua was able to *give* orders because he'd learned how to *take* orders.

Because he was submitted to authority, Joshua was an obedient servant. During the first half of his life, he obeyed Moses; and during the last half, he received his orders from the Lord. The key verse in Joshua's life was, "Be careful to obey all the law My servant Moses gave you; do not turn from it to the right or to the left, that you may be successful wherever you go" (Josh. 1:7, NIV). This should be balanced with 11:15, "As the Lord commanded Moses, his servant, so did Moses command Joshua, and so did Joshua; he left nothing undone of all that the Lord commanded Moses."

Delay. It's through faith and patience that we inherit what God has promised (Heb. 6:12). Had the people of Israel listened to Joshua and Caleb, they would have entered their inheritance four decades sooner and enjoyed it that much longer (Num. 13:26–14:10). Both Joshua and Caleb patiently endured the trials of the wilderness because they knew they would one day claim their inheritance in the Promised Land. In their unbelief, the Jews rejected "the work of faith" and refused to enter the land; but they couldn't rob Joshua of his "patience of hope" (1 Thes. 1:3).

Leaders must learn how to wait. Often their followers don't always see as far as they see or have the faith that they have. The vision of future victory is what motivates a true leader; but, like Israel, too often the people are looking back. I suppose every leader has at one time or another identified with Jesus when He said, "O unbelieving and perverse generation, how long shall I stay with you and put up with you?" (Luke 9:41, NIV) On more than one occasion Joshua witnessed Moses pouring out his heart to God because of the unbelief and stubbornness of the people.

2. Joshua's leadership

Are leaders born or made? Probably both. God gives them the genetic structure they need and then develops their gifts and abilities in the "school of life." Management seminars promise to teach *leadership;* but if there isn't some fuel there to ignite, the fire won't burn. Principles of leadership certainly may be taught, but what it means to be a leader can only be learned on the field of action. To think you're a leader because you attended a seminar is as dangerous as thinking you're an athlete because you watched the Olympics on television.

What were the characteristics of Joshua's leadership style?

He walked with God. Like Moses, his predecessor, Joshua was a man of God. Whoever the Holy Spirit selected to complete the Book of Joshua was led to call him "the servant of the Lord," a title not given to everybody in Scripture. We aren't told that God spoke with Joshua face to face, as He had with Moses (Deut. 34:10); but we do know that God communicated His will to Joshua and that he was obedient. Joshua meditated daily on the Law of the Lord (Josh. 1:8) and did what it said (11:15). He was a man of prayer (7:6-9), for the Word of God and prayer go together (Acts 6:4).

He had courage. At the beginning of his ministry Joshua was told four times to "be courageous" (Josh. 1:6-7, 9, 18). It takes courage to be a successful leader, courage to stand for what you believe, and courage to do what you know God wants you to do. All of us need to imitate Martin Luther when he said, "Here I stand. I can do no other."

General Omar Bradley defined bravery as "the capacity to perform properly even when scared half to death." We aren't told whether Joshua was ever afraid as he faced the enemy, but we do know that he did his job and won battle after battle. Most of us aren't called upon to lead armies, but any kind of leadership involves risks and demands moral courage. "He who loves his life will lose it, and he who hates his life in this world will keep it for eternal life" (John 12:25, NKJV). If we're timid about life and ministry, we'll never accomplish much for the Lord. It was because the servant was afraid that he hid his master's wealth and didn't take the risk of investing it (Matt. 25:24-30).

But Joshua's courage involved much more than fighting the enemy, as great as that was. He also had the courage to deal with sin in the camp of Israel (Josh. 7) and to challenge the tribes to "get with it" and claim their inheritance (17:14-18). Sometimes it takes more courage to face your own people at home than it takes to face the enemy on the battlefield.

He had a plan and followed it. The conquest of Canaan wasn't a haphazard affair; it was carefully planned and skillfully executed. First, Joshua cut straight across the land and isolated the north from the south. Then he conquered the cities in the south, followed by the invasion of the north. He moved quickly to subdue the population centers and take control of the whole land. More than once, Joshua led his men on an all-night march in order to catch the enemy by surprise.

It takes planning and strategy to do the work of the Lord successfully. The leader who drifts with the tide and changes direction with every new wind isn't a leader at all. A Roman proverb says, "When the pilot doesn't know what port he's heading for, no wind is the right wind." If you know where you're going, you can adjust your sails when the storm starts to blow and still arrive at the right port.

He didn't quit. When he was defeated at Ai, Joshua admitted failure, sought the face of the Lord, went back, and won the battle. When he foolishly made a league with the Gibeonites, he admitted his mistake and put it to work for him. The successful leader isn't the one who is always right, because no such person exists. Successful leaders are people who make the best decisions they can and keep on going when they make mistakes. They learn from their mistakes and know how to snatch victory out of defeat.

The American humorist Elbert Hubbard said, "Experience is the name everyone gives his mistakes." Someone has said that experience is a tough teacher because it always gives the exam first and teaches the lesson afterward. If we turn our mistakes into mirrors, we'll see only ourselves; and this will make us miserable. But if by faith we turn our mistakes into windows, we'll see the Lord and get the strength we need to try again. To quote Elbert Hubbard again: "There is no failure except in no longer trying."

He enlisted others and commanded their respect. Except for Achan, the traitor at Jericho, and Caleb, the man of faith, we don't know the names of any of the soldiers who served with Joshua; *but he couldn't have done the job without them.* The conquest of Canaan wasn't the work of one man; it was the work of thousands of people who served faithfully in the battle and behind the lines.

True leaders don't *demand* respect; they *command* it. When you read Joshua 1:10-18 and see the way the troops responded to Joshua's orders, you can't help but conclude that he commanded their respect and loyalty. He was serving the Lord and the Lord's people, and they followed him because they knew they could trust him. His motives were pure, his life was godly, and his character was above reproach.

As Moses' successor and God's appointed leader, Joshua had *authority;* but it takes more than authority to lead others. It also takes *stature,* the kind of character and achievement that will make people look up to you and listen to you. In this day of "media magic," a public relations firm can "hype" a nobody into becoming an international celebrity; but they can't give that celebrity the kind of stature that can come only from sacrifice and service. We don't need more celebrities, but we certainly do need more servants.

Real leaders don't use people to build their authority; they use their authority to build people. Many a soldier in the Jewish army became a hero because Joshua was in command. A true leader is one who leaves behind people who have achieved far more than they would have achieved had they not followed his or her leadership.

He was concerned about the future. When King Hezekiah was told that the kingdom of Judah would eventually go into captivity in Babylon, his response was, "At least there will be peace and truth in my days" (Isa. 39:8, NKJV). I don't want to be critical of a great king, but this statement seems to reek of selfishness. Isn't a king supposed to be concerned about the generations to come?

Joshua's two farewell speeches (chaps. 23–24) give ample evidence that he was a true leader, burdened for the future of his country. He wanted to be sure that the people knew the Lord and wanted to serve Him with their whole heart. People who think only of what they can get today are only opportunists and not true leaders. Leadership means planting the right seeds that will bear fruit in years to come for the benefit of others, and Joshua did that.

He glorified God. There was a time in Joshua's life when he was jealous for the honor of his master, Moses (Num. 11:24-30); but he learned that the most important thing was the glory of the Lord. When the nation crossed the Jordan, it was God who received the glory. "By this you shall know that the living God is among you!" he told the people (Josh. 3:10, NKJV). When that miracle march was over, Joshua put up a monument so that Israel and "all the peoples of the earth may know the hand of the Lord, that it is mighty" (4:24, NKJV). A lesser man would have put up a monument glorifying himself.

As you read the book that Joshua wrote, you see that he repeatedly gave God the glory for all that happened (6:16; 8:1; 10:14; 11:6-8; 13:6; 18:3; 21:43-45). It was the Lord who conquered the enemy and gave the land to the people. It was the name of the Lord that was to be magnified in all the earth. It has been said that a leader is somebody who takes twice as much blame and half as much credit, and Joshua would qualify on both counts.

3. Joshua's message

The practical message of the Book of Joshua is that God keeps His promises and enables His servants to succeed if they will trust Him and obey His Word. The spiritual message is that God has a rich inheritance for His children *now*, and they can claim it by faith. This message is amplified in the Book of Hebrews, especially chapters 3 and 4.

We have seen that, when it comes to the things of the Lord, there are several different kinds of people in this world. Most people are still in bondage in Egypt and need to be delivered by faith in Jesus Christ. Others have trusted Christ and been delivered from bondage but are wandering in the wilderness of unbelief because they won't enter into their inheritance by faith. Still others have "sampled" the inheritance but prefer to live on the borders of the blessing. Finally, there are those who follow their Joshua (Jesus = "Jehovah is salvation") and enter the Promised Land and claim their inheritance.

Remember, crossing the Jordan and entering the land is not a picture of dying and going to heaven. It's a picture of dying to self and the old life and entering our spiritual inheritance here and now, enjoying the fullness of God's blessing as we serve the Lord and glorify Him. It's what Hebrews 4 and 5 call "entering into His rest."

The greatest need in the church today is for God's people to see how much they are missing by wandering in unbelief, or by living on the borderline of the blessing, and then to claim God's promises and enter into their spiritual inheritance. We're a deprived people because we've failed to claim our spiritual riches; and we're a defeated people because we've failed to trust our Joshua to lead us on to victory. Too many of us are like Achan, stealing from God, when we ought to be like Caleb, claiming the mountains and overcoming the giants.

4. Joshua's God

The Lord, not Joshua, is the key Person in this book. As you read the Book of Joshua, you discover many wonderful truths about God.

To begin with, He is the God of His people Israel, the God of the covenant that He made with Israel through Moses. Though Moses was dead, the living God was still at work in and through His chosen people. When Joshua commanded the people, he often called God "the Lord your God." Israel belonged to Him.

But He is also "the Lord of all the earth" (Josh. 3:11). While He has a special relationship to Israel, He established that relationship in order to bring His blessing to all the nations (Gen. 12:1-3). The pagan nations in Canaan heard about what God had done for Israel, and they were frightened (Josh. 2:10-11); for none of their gods had ever done such mighty deeds.

He is the God who keeps His promises. He had promised the fathers of the Jewish nation that He would give them their land, and He kept His promise. He had promised Moses that Israel would drive out the nations in Canaan and defeat them, and He kept that promise too. At the close of his life Joshua was able to say to his people that not one thing had failed of all the good things that the Lord their God spoke concerning them (23:14).

He is a holy God who will not tolerate sin. When Achan disobeyed the ban that God had put on Jericho, God withdrew His blessing. The army of Israel was defeated at Ai, and they could not expect victory until Joshua dealt with the sin in the camp. But He is also a forgiving God who cleanses us when we confess our sins, and then gives us another opportunity for victory.

He is a God who requires obedience on the part of His people. Before Israel could enter the land, they had to submit to the requirements that God had laid down; for they were His covenant people. The Lord told Joshua that the secret of his success would be faith and obedience to the Word of God. God had a plan for the conquest of the land; all Joshua had to do was obey that plan.

He is the God who never fails! We may fail Him, but He will never fail us. "When God ordains our service," wrote J. Oswald Sanders, "He is morally obligated to see us through" (*Robust in Faith,* p. 72).

Although much more could be said, let's close on this note: He is a God who is gracious. In view of the fact that thousands of people were slain during the conquest of Canaan, it may seem strange to think about God's grace; but the grace of God was there just the same. God was gracious to delay His judgment for centuries before bringing Israel into the land (Gen. 15:16). He was gracious to send the reports about Israel into the land so that the people could fear and, like Rahab, turn to the Lord. He was gracious to wipe out the filthy religion of the Canaanites so that the Jewish boys and girls could grow up in a land where Jehovah was honored and worshiped.

When I was about to graduate from seminary, our class went on a weekend retreat; and for one of his messages, the speaker used Joshua 3:5 as his text: "Sanctify yourselves: for tomorrow the Lord will do wonders among you." I've forgotten the outline, but I remember the message: Our tomorrows can be exciting and wonderful if we are all that God wants us to be.

He is still the God of wonders, and He is still calling us to be a sanctified people who will trust and obey. The God of Joshua lives—but where are the Joshuas?